Pottery
Step-by-Step

Pottery
Step-by-Step

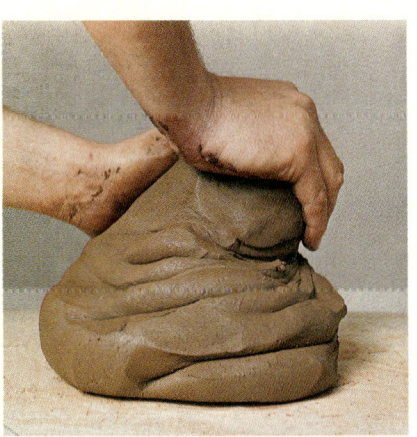

Collier Books
A Division of Macmillan Publishing Co., Inc.
New York

738.1
P85

A Studio Vista book published by
Cassell & Collier Macmillan Publishers Ltd.,
35 Red Lion Square, London WC1R 4SG,
and at Sydney, Auckland, Toronto, Johannesburg,
an affiliate of Macmillan, Inc., New York

Copyright © Studio Vista, a division
of Cassell and Collier Macmillan Publishers
Ltd., 1976
First published in the U.K. by Studio Vista,
a division of Cassell and Collier Macmillan
Publishers Ltd.
First Collier Books Edition 1976

All rights reserved. No part of this
book may be reproduced or
transmitted in any form or by any means,
electronic or mechanical, including
photocopying, recording or by any
information storage and retrieval system
without permission in writing from the
Publisher.

Macmillan Publishing Co., Inc.
866 Third Avenue, New York, N.Y. 10022

Library of Congress Cataloguing in Publication Data
Main entry under title:
Pottery step-by-step.
"A Studio Vista book."
1. Pottery craft.
TT920.P63 1976b   738.1   76-8826
ISBN 0-02-011810-4

Printed in The Netherlands

Contents

Introduction to Pottery	7
Clay Preparation	8
Pinch Pots	10
Coiled Pots	12
Slab Pots	14
Moulded Dishes and Pots	16
Slip Cast Forms	19
Carved Forms	22
Thrown Cylinder and Bottle	24
Thrown Bowl	27
Trimming Thrown Forms	29
Composite Thrown Forms	31
Hanging Planter	33
Jug and Teapot	34
Oxides	37
Surface Decoration	40
Slip Decoration	42
Inlaid Decoration	46
The Damp Cupboard and Drying	48
Packing and Firing the Kiln	49
Glazes and Glost firing	52
The Sawdust Kiln	58
Enamels and Beads	60
Storage and Reconstitution of Clay	63
List of Suppliers	64
Some Further Reading	64

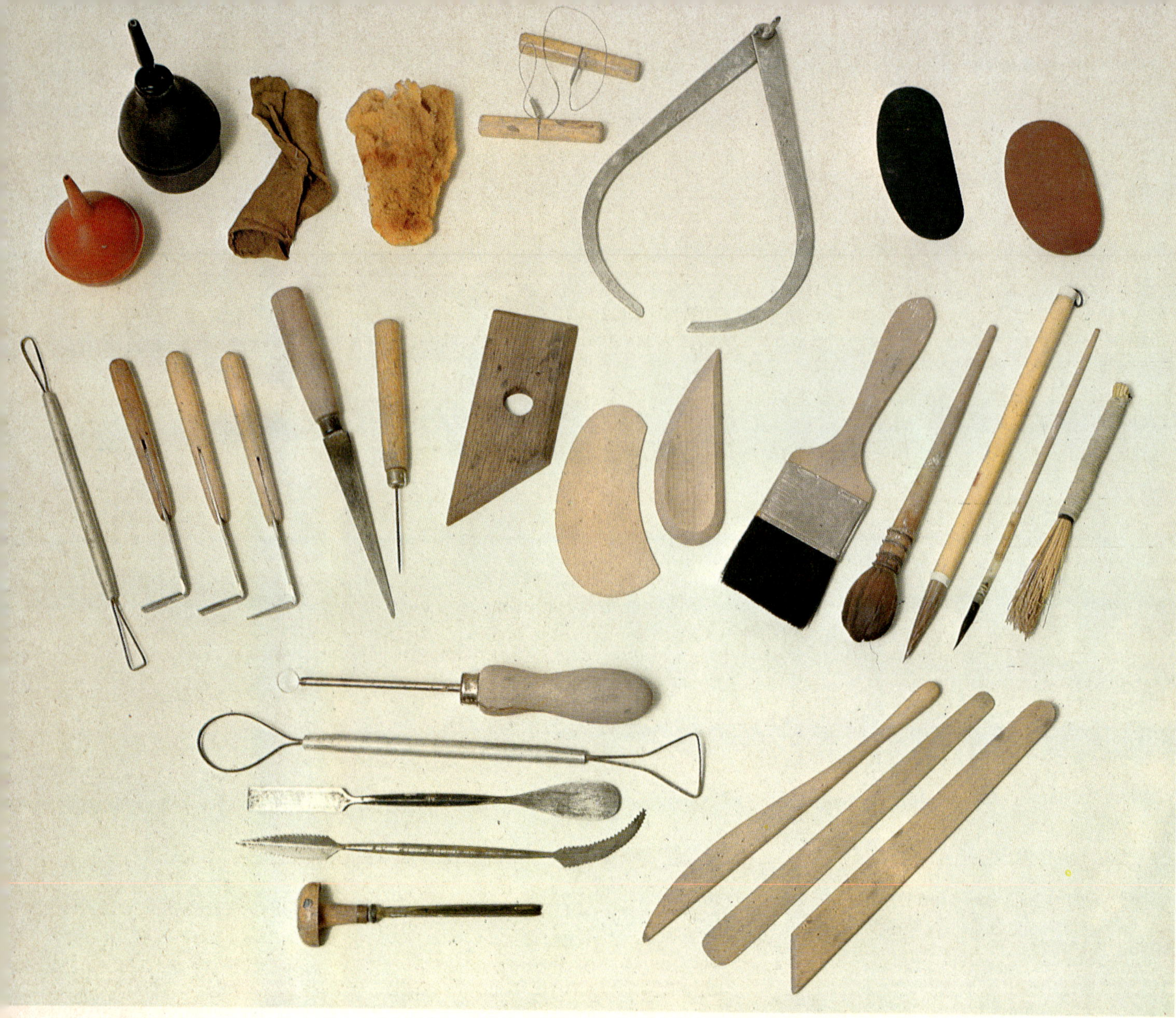

Introduction to pottery

All the general purpose tools and equipment you will need to make the projects in this book. Numbers in brackets refer to pages where they are introduced and you can find out more about them. From left to right (top row): *Slip trailers* (42). *Chamois leather* and *'elephant ear' sponge* – needed for throwing (24). *Potter's wire. Calipers* – for measuring thrown forms (31). *Steel and rubber palettes or scrapers.* (Middle row) *Clay turning tools* – you will need a selection of profiles. *Potter's knife* and *potter's pin* – essential equipment. *Wooden ribs* – for throwing. *Brushes* – for decoration (42) and for kiln wash (49). (Bottom row) *Turning, carving and plaster working tools. Fine gouge* – for mishima (46). *Wooden modelling tools* – a selection is useful.

A selection of typical plastic containers and utensils suitable for pottery use. Sieves and a stiff brush, a banding wheel and an accurate weigh scale are among the most commonly used equipment in small studios.

Pottery is perhaps the most appealing of all the crafts and certainly the most widely practised. Since the infancy of our species it has played a fundamental role in providing practical utensils for everyday life, as well as being one of the richest vehicles for the expression of man's artistic impulses.

Two aspects of pottery make it particularly attractive to the beginner. Firstly, you do not have to wait for years to experience a measure of success. Because the processes of pottery are, in essence, such simple ones there is no reason why you should not be pleased with even your first efforts. What is vital is that you should learn carefully the disciplines, possibilities and limitations of each new process. As your projects become more varied or ambitious, you will develop your general understanding of the craft. The second great appeal of pottery is its cheapness. Clay and most other basic ceramic materials are inexpensive to buy and you can, if you wish, supplement these with materials you glean from nature. Tools and equipment also need not be expensive: most potters prefer homemade or simple tools and the studio equipment you require depends upon the project you plan to tackle.

Many people like to begin pottery by joining a class or club where a variety of materials and equipment are available. In this way you can experiment and find which are most suited to your needs and preferences before you buy.

This book offers you a series of projects which allow you to learn most of the basic processes of pottery. It shows you how to decorate and glaze your work and also how to prepare, pack and fire the most common types of electric kiln with safety and efficiency. But, perhaps more importantly, it demonstrates that working with pottery is enjoyable, satisfying and exciting and lays sound foundations in the craft that will allow you to move on to more advanced and ambitious work.

Clay Preparation

1 Working on a firm surface, press with the heels of both hands into the rear of the mass.

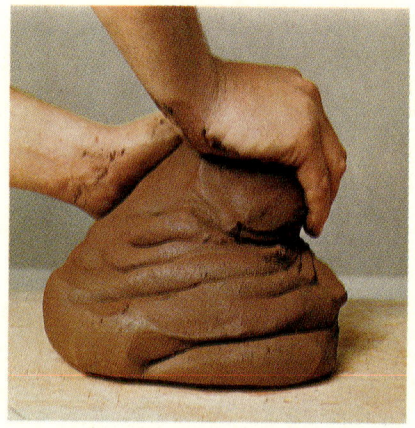

2 Follow with a twisting and compressing action in which pressure from one hand predominates.

3 Spread grog on the work surface. Knead the clay on it until all has been absorbed.

You will need:
Plaster slab
Potter's wire
Grog
Damp cloth or plastic sheeting

The basic material from which all pottery objects are made is clay. Clays are earth minerals which have been derived by the processes of weathering and hydrothermal degradation of igneous rocks. Millions of years of erosion have reduced the mother rock to extremely fine lamellar particles, which have either been deposited in beds on the site of their formation or have been carried by wind and water to be laid down elsewhere as strata within the earth's crust.

Soil is often erroneously thought of as clay and indeed does contain some clay; but since it is heavily polluted with humus, sand and stones it is useless for pottery. Clay is to be found in the earth in the subsoil stratas and, while it is perfectly possible – even desirable – to dig your own clay from nature, it is normal and much more convenient for the beginner to buy a ready prepared product from a clay supplier. Most suppliers (see page 64) will send you a copy of their catalogue on request. These are well worth obtaining for, besides providing you with information about the individual products which you are interested in buying, they are a source of data and reference material.

Most studio pottery is made from clay which is mixed with just sufficient water to make it malleable. This water, known as pore water, serves the dual purposes of helping to bind the particles together yet at the same time provides lubrication between them so that we have a material which is at one and the same time strong – in the sense that it does not fall apart – and easily modelled and manipulated. The ability of clay to be easily shaped and to retain this shape as it dries is known as 'plasticity' and is the most important characteristic of clay.

The other important characteristic of clay is its reaction to fire. All clays are affected by the application of heat; firstly becoming hard and rocklike but later, if overfired, they soften and eventually melt. The temperature at which a given clay obtains its optimum qualities of strength and resonance is called the maturation temperature.

There are three main categories of clay product:

Earthenwares – potteries maturing at 1100°C (2012°F) or less.

Stonewares – potteries maturing between 1200–1300°C (2282–2372°F).

Porcelain – potteries maturing at above 1300°C (2372°F)

Although several clay types occur in nature only a few are used alone. Normally a number of clays are blended in a carefully designed composition (called a 'clay body') to give optimum working qualities and maturation temperature.

Earthenware clay bodies are those which contain large amounts of easily fusible components, stoneware bodies contain those fluxing agents active at higher temperatures, while porcelain is based on unpolluted china clay and high temperature fluxes. A basic relationship exists, therefore, between the clay with which you work and the temperature to which the piece will eventually be fired.

Pottery suppliers normally sell clays by weight in one of the following forms.

A Plastic Clay Body – a clay blend suitable for a particular firing temperature range, mixed and ready for use. This is the most convenient way to buy, but at least 20% of what you buy is water.

Dry Clay Powder – separated and refined individual clays for use by potters who prefer to design and compound clay bodies to suit their individual needs.

Clay Slip – a suspension of clay particles in water. Slips are easy to make but you may prefer to buy an industrial product if you are contemplating slip casting on some scale.

Clay for use in pottery then needs to be of the type suitable for the processing intended for it and to be easily malleable without being sticky or unworkably soft. If your clay is too wet spread it out on a wooden board or a slab of plaster of Paris until the excess water has been absorbed. If, on the other hand, the clay is too stiff cut it into thin slices with a potter's wire, moisten each face with a wet sponge and knead the pieces of clay back together into a single mass. Repeat the process if necessary. Finally, the clay needs to be homogenous, the water content must be uniform throughout the mass and all air bubbles must be removed. This is achieved by kneading.

Although kneading is a two-handed, manipulative process, the real work is done by the weight of the torso and the shoulders, so the surface upon which you work should be at about thigh height. Try to think of your fingers as being joined together: do not let them separate during the kneading process or they will dig into the clay and create pockets to trap air. Do not try to knead too much clay at one time until you have learned the technique.

Some projects recommend the addition of grog (ground fire brick) to your clay (see page 14). Combine this with the clay as part of the kneading process (see **3**).

Test the progress of your kneading by cutting through the clay mass with your potter's wire. No marbled traces of constituents or air bubbles should be evident. Bring the two pieces of clay together again sharply with the full weight of the body behind the action in order to exclude air. Wrap in a damp cloth or plastic sheeting if it is not for immediate use.

4 Mix two different clays by slicing each mass and intersupersing one with the other. Knead.

5 Cut through with a wire. A marbled pattern clearly indicates an insufficiently kneaded mixture.

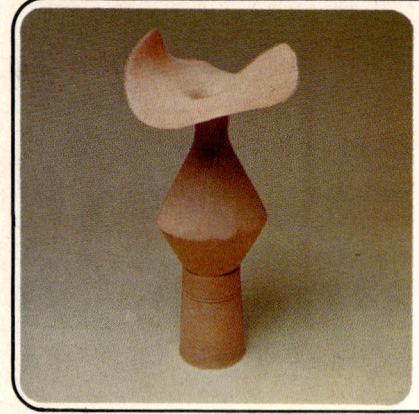

Pinch Pots

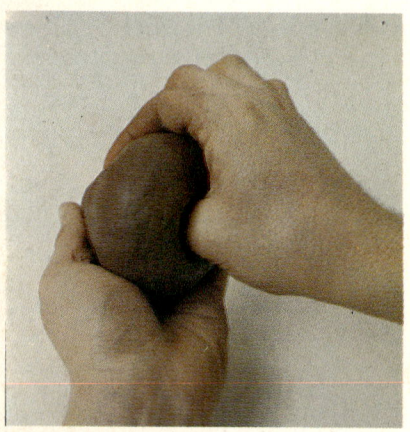

1 Push the right thumb into the centre of the clay. Thin walls by pinching between thumb and fingers.

2 Thin the form from the base upwards. Consolidate the lip; moisten it slightly if cracks appear.

3 Use a potter's pin to score the lips of each component. Apply coats of thick slip to each.

4 Press the modules together so that slip is exuded. Use your finger or a tool to weld the joins.

You will need:
Fine, plastic clay
Potter's pin
Slip
Brush
Wooden paddle
Scrapers

Pinching small pots from balls of clay, using only the fingers as tools, is one of the most ancient of pottery techniques. Although it can be thought of as being the simplest pottery forming technique it is capable of exhibiting refined and subtle qualities.

The clay for making pinch pots should be fine in texture and of good plasticity. It must not dry out too quickly from contact with the hands and must not be prone to cracking or tearing. A plastic earthenware body containing about 15% of the finest grog is ideal. It should be in a very malleable condition without being sticky and must be well kneaded.

The bowl is the normal product of the pinching process. Cylindrical shapes can be made, but conical ones are preferred. More complex forms, such as the bottle shown here, are made by joining two or more basic bowl modules.

Correct action by the two hands

during the pinching process is the key to success. The left hand has two simultaneous functions to perform. Firstly, the whole hand has to be held in such a way that it both cradles and supports the shape of the developing form. Secondly, it has to turn the form constantly so that it may be thinned and modelled as it passes through the right hand. The right hand is used exclusively for thinning and shaping the walls. Keep the fingers together and thin the walls with a gentle squeezing action between them and the thumb.

5 Use a piece of wood to beat the pot gently into shape before cutting open the neck orifice.

An optimum thickness of wall for pinch pots is 5mm ($\frac{1}{4}$in.) or less. Model the whole of the bowl within the supporting cradle of the left hand (see **2**).

Cracks in the walls are usually the result of poor technique, but this can also be caused by the clay drying out too quickly. In this latter case cover the pot with a damp cloth for a few minutes, smooth over the cracks with the fingers and continue pinching.

Model the lip of the bowl with care; damp it lightly if it has a tendency to crack and strengthen it by compressing it gently with the index finger while supporting the walls with the thumb and second finger.

When finished, bowls should be stood on their base so as not to mar the lip. Pieces that are to be components in bottle forms may be stood on their lips to stiffen.

In order to make the bottle illustrated, model up three basic bowl forms. The first two will be joined lip to lip to form the belly of the pot (so they need to be of the same diameter). The third will be joined foot to foot with the inverted second element and re-pinched *in situ* to form the wide flaring lip.

6 Support the upper component carefully as you refine its shape into a decorative form.

7 When the whole pot has stiffened scrape down its surface to reveal the final form.

Pinch up all three bowl forms on the same occasion and from the same batch of clay. Allow the first two to stiffen in the air for a few hours but keep the third slightly softer by covering it loosely with plastic sheeting.

Mix some of the clay body with a little water until it is reduced to a slip the consistency of thick cream – this is used an adhesive in joining the clay modules. Leave the pot to stiffen overnight before cutting the neck aperture through into the belly of the pot.

When the basic forming of the pots is complete keep it uncovered in the damp cupboard for a few days, as a result of which it will have stiffened to a largely inflexible condition (termed 'leather-hard'). The surface of the pot can now be finally refined by being cut, pared down and scraped. Surform tools, hacksaw blades and scrapers made from pieces of flexible metal are all suitable for this task. Finally, if you wish, you can burnish all or part of the surface of the pot with the back of a spoon.

Handle the pot with increasing care as it dries, since it becomes extremely brittle after the leather-hard condition.

Coiled Pots

You will need:
Plastic clay
Wooden board or bat
Knife or potter's pin
Wooden paddle
Surform tools
Scraper

The technique of building up pieces of pottery from coils of clay is very ancient. It does not require such precisely disciplined manipulation as the pinch pot (page 10) but it is vigorous and direct and it allows us to build up very large forms comparatively quickly and easily. Coil building may be used to make pots of any shape, but its most common application is to produce large, asymmetric forms. (Symmetrical forms are much more easily produced by other methods.)

Clay for coil building may be of any of the common body types, provided that it is reasonably plastic. Generally it should include 10-15% mixed fine and medium grades of grog (although for very large pots, such as this, increase this amount by a few percent and include larger grades of grog). Make the clay up to a fairly soft consistency, since rolling the coils tends to dry it considerably.

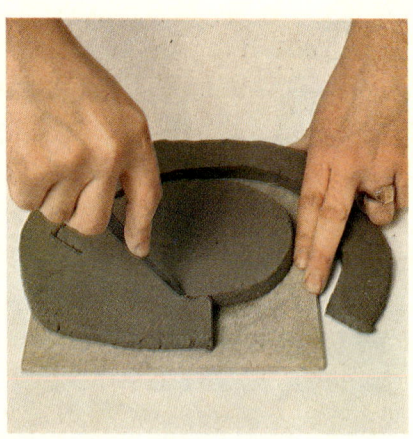

1 Cut a base of appropriate size and shape from a slab of clay approximately 19 mm (¾ in.) thick.

Knead the clay thoroughly before you start work.

It is best to build your pot on a bat (see page 25) or wooden board so that it can be turned and moved as necessary. If you have access to a bench banding wheel (see page 6) use this to carry the bat or board.

It is desirable to have a fairly well evolved visualization of the shape you plan to make before you begin.

Start by making the base of the pot (see **1**, page 14). Then make up a whole batch of coils at one time before going on to use them. The coils should be about 25mm

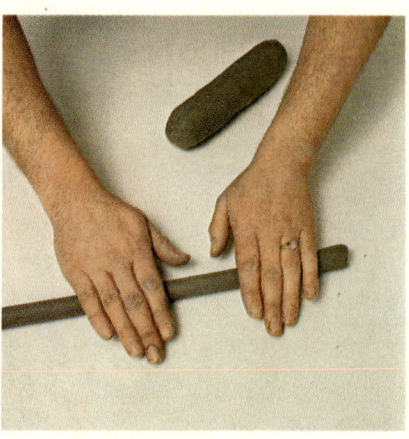

2 Roll out the coils. Apply only moderate pressure and use the full areas of the hands.

(1in.) thick and completely round. Wrap them in plastic sheeting as they are made to keep them damp and malleable until they are needed.

Begin making the pot by scoring the perimeter of the top surface of the base with a potter's pin or the tip of a knife. Apply a coat of thick slip and place the first coil on this prepared area, pressing it down well. Cut off any excess coil and join the two cut ends together carefully to form a complete ring.

Secure the first coil to the base within the pot by pushing down a little of the clay from the coil and

3 Use a finger to press down a little clay from the coil and weld it securely to the base.

4 Stagger the joins in subsequent coils. After adding several coils weld together on interior.

5 Weld coils together in the same way on the exterior before continuing to build the pit.

welding it into the clay forming the base.

The second coil is joined to the top of the first and the two welded together on the interior surface. It is not essential to apply slip between coils although some potters prefer to do so. Do not allow joins in coils to be located vertically above one another as this creates a line of weakness within the wall of the pot. If the form of the pot is intended to belly out as it rises add each coil slightly towards the outer edge of its predecessor. In convergent forms coils are added a little towards the inner edge of the one beneath.

After about eight coils have been added, weld over the joins and adjust or consolidate the shape if necessary, paddling the walls with a piece of wood (**6**). When making large pots, particularly when they are divergent in shape, it is best to allow them to stiffen in the air over night at this stage to prevent the form from slumping. Before setting it aside, however, it is advisable to wrap a strip of damp cloth around the top coil and to cover this with a strip of plastic sheeting. When you resume work on the piece, score the lip with a potter's pin and

6 As the form progresses use a wooden paddle to beat the clay walls into the desired profile.

7 Refine the surface of the completed pot with surform tools and finally scrapers.

apply slip before you add further coils.

The forming procedure then continues until the full height of the pot is achieved, at which point in time the whole piece should be encased in plastic sheeting and left in the damp cupboard (see page 48) for a minimum of 24 hours so that moisture can equalize throughout the piece and thus reduce drying strains.

You can then undertake the final shaping of the piece by further paddling. Use shaped paddles to obtain special profiles. Do not try to alter the form too radically or too quickly and allow the clay to settle between short sessions of paddling.

Should you wish to have a neck or high relief surface decoration on your pot this should be coiled or added onto the form after the general shape has been achieved, followed by another session in the damp cupboard.

The final refinement of the surface of the pot is not undertaken until the whole piece is of leather-hard consistency, when it may be planed, cut, scraped or textured as required.

Slab Pots

You will need:
Clay and grog
Large piece of cloth or sacking
2 spacing sticks
Large rolling pin
Knife or potter's pin
Slip
Scraper

The construction of pots and ceramic sculptures from flat slabs of clay is one of the most popular of the hand building processes.

There are two main problems encountered in making slab pots: the joins between the slabs tend to split open and the flat sides of the form tend to warp and distort. Insufficient care taken when making the joins and strains set up by uncontrolled drying account for the first of these. The second is the result of poor technique or due to an unsuitable clay body.

Grog
The material made from crushed fire brick and known to potters as 'grog' is one of the most useful components that can be included in a clay body.

There are a number of valuable characteristics which grog imparts. It opens up compact clay bodies and promotes trouble-free,

1 Turn the clay frequently during rolling. Use spacing sticks to achieve desired thickness.

2 Draw the shapes of each component part onto stiff card and use these as templates for cutting the clay.

3 Score the site of each join and apply coats of thick slip before luting the slabs together.

4 Weld the slabs firmly together. Join a thin coil of clay into each interior corner of the pot.

The slab-building technique can be applied to the production of a variety of flat faced forms.

easy and rapid drying. Because grog is pre-fired it reduces the overall shrinkage during drying and firing. It also facilitates successful joining of clay components and minimizes warping.

Up to 30% grog may be added to a body for slab building, but it is suggested that you start with about 20% for this first project, composed of equal amounts of fine, medium and coarse grades.

Begin with a fairly plastic red clay or mix some red earthenware clay into a stoneware body to give it some colour. Combine the grog with the clay as described on page 8.

This table garden is a deep, sheer-sided tray made from five slabs of clay raised on a simple rectangular foot made from four more clay strips. The five slabs should be made in a single session to minimize differences in consistency and moisture content.

When the basic form has been made wrap the whole construction, on its board, in plastic sheeting (see page 48) and leave it in the damp cupboard for at least 24 hours to allow moisture to equalize throughout the piece. After this period remove the plastic sheeting and allow the piece to stiffen in the damp cupboard till it has achieved a leather-hard condition. Return the piece to the damp cupboard after the foot has been added.

You need only glaze the inside of the piece so it is waterproof. The natural, rock-like surface of the unglazed exterior will look right as it is.

Colour can be added through the use of colour slips or a wash or light spray of metallic oxide mixed in water (see page 37).

5 When the pot is leather-hard lute on the slabs which form the foot. Score and apply slip to all joins.

6 When the whole pot has stiffened uniformly scrape down the exterior walls and corners.

Moulded Dishes and Pots

1 Draw the shape of the mould on a piece of board. Use scrap clay to make an inverted model of the form.

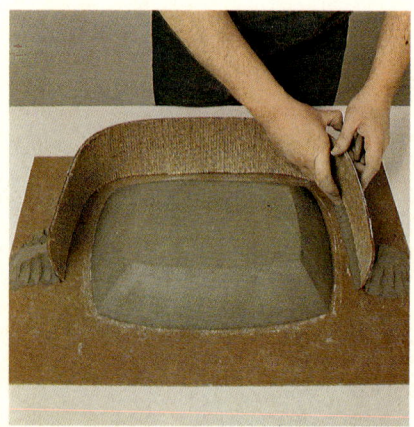

2 Construct a strong retaining wall around the model. Seal all joins with clay.

You will need:
Piece of board
Scrap clay and plastic clay with grog
Sieve
Bucket
Plaster of Paris
Newspaper
Strip of linoleum
String
Scrapers and surform tools
Rolling pin and spacing sticks
Sponge
Potter's wire
Rubber scraper
Plastic sheeting
Potter's pin
Slip

Plaster of Paris moulds are much used, both in studio and industrial pottery, for the production of moulded or cast clay forms.

The press mould detailed here will allow you to make moulded dishes, moulded pots and relief or free-standing sculptures.

The mould is made by covering a clay model of the form required with plaster of Paris. The model can be regular or asymmetric in shape, but keep it fairly simple for your first effort. Size, again, is a matter for your personal choice, but a maximum

3 To make plaster, sieve dry plaster and sprinkle evenly over water till no free water remains.

4 Mix by hand to disperse lumps. Allow to stand until first signs of stiffening then pour immediately.

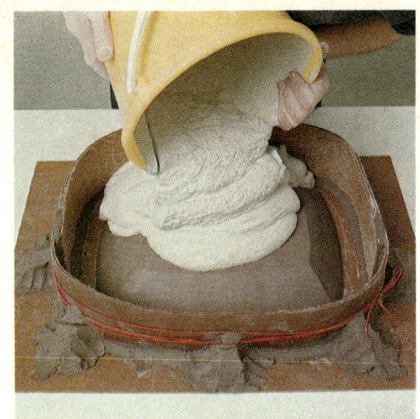

5 Pour plaster over the highest point of the model so that it flows down to cover all its modulations.

6 When the plaster has set remove wall. Scrape down any irregularities on exterior of mould.

7 Invert mould and remove board. Release the clay model. Scrape down imperfections in the cast.

dimension of about 38-46cm (15-18ins) is suggested.

Do not under any circumstances wash the remains of the plaster down the sink.

Put aside the clay used in mould making for future use. Never return clay polluted with fragments of plaster to your general clay stock.

Now that we have one or more press moulds, we are able to consider some of their possible applications to pottery.

PRESSED DISHES

The most basic application of the press mould is in producing dishes.

Pressed dishes are made from rolled out slabs of clay and any plastic clay body which contains 10-30% of grog will be suitable. (Use a fine grade of grog if you want a smooth surface on the dish.

Roll out the clay (see page 14) until it is several inches larger than the mould in all dimensions. Lower the clay into the mould and trim off the surplus.

Polish the interior surface of the dish and refine the shape of the lip with a damp sponge and a rubber kidney.

Leave the dish in the mould to

8 Roll out clay slab. Lower it carefully into the mould. Use a moist sponge to press into recesses.

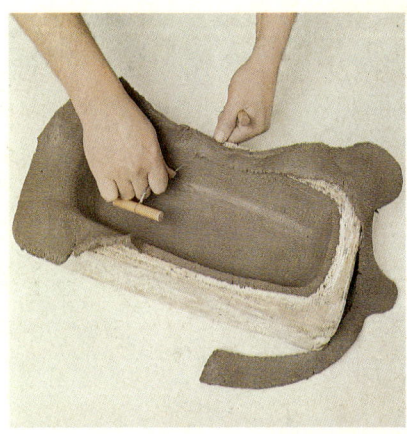

9 Trim off surplus clay which projects above the face of the mould. Refine the lip.

10 Remove the semi-stiff dish from the mould by inverting it onto a board. Enclose in plastic sheet.

11 Score both lips with a potter's pin. Apply several applications of thick slip to scored areas.

12 Leave one dish in the mould. Join on the other lip-to-lip. Use a tool to weld the two forms together.

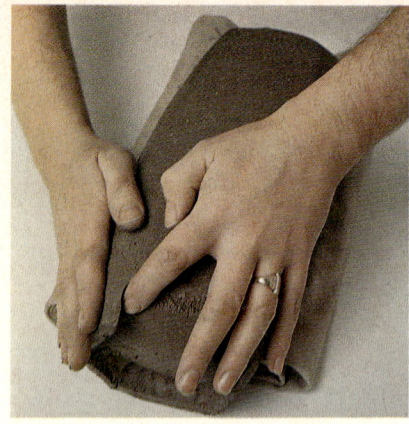

13 Weld slabs onto prepared areas of the pot to form a foot. Paddle them into line with the pot walls.

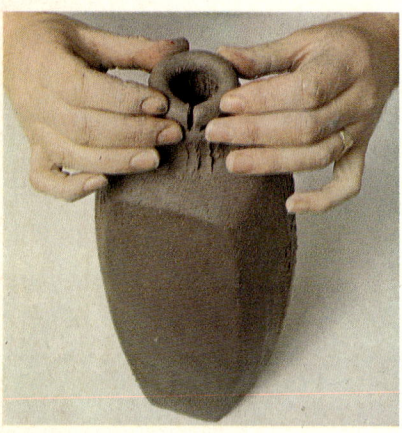

14 Pierce a neck orifice through into the pot and coil up a suitable neck form around it.

15 When the whole piece has become leather-hard refine the surface by planing or scraping.

CERAMIC MURALS OR WALL SCULPTURES

Attractive relief wall murals or wall sculptures can be made from basic modules formed in press moulds. While the clay is still fairly soft and supported by the mould, penetrations can be cut through the walls of the dish, shapes removed or pared back, parts of the dish wall bent to change the basic profile and decorative walls, partitions, bridges or projections cut from additional clay slabs can be luted onto the interior surface of the form (see page 40).

A number of these units may be laced together, attached to a panel with epoxy resin cement or cemented into a wall to form a large scale sculptural relief panel.

MOULDED POTS

Large, unusual and exciting pots can be produced from a single press mould. Two moulded dishes are joined lip to lip, paddled into shape and completed by the addition of a neck and foot.

Final shaping of the piece is effected by planing and scraping.

Finally, the neck opening can be cut and a suitable tool inserted to weld over the main interior join between the two dishes.

FREE-STANDING SCULPTURES

Constructions of this type are made in the same manner as the moulded pots just described, except that a number of press moulds are employed to yield moulded slabs having a variety of profiles and curvatures. It is, of course, not necessary to use the moulded dish shapes whole. They can be cut into suitable components before or after being removed from the mould and used as you please in a wide variety of combinations.

stiffen overnight and remove it the next day.

Scrape or plane the exterior of the form, should it be necessary, with the dish in an inverted position. It may be turned right way up when it is leather-hard in order to refine the lip or to add decoration to the interior, but it should be turned back onto its lip, preferably on a slatted shelf, to dry. In this way severe warping is usually avoided.

Glazes which suggest the action of natural process offset the geometry of this moulded bottle.

Slip Cast Forms

1 Pour casting slip into the centre of the mould until it stands up slightly above the face of the plaster.

2 When a suitable deposit of slip has been found on the walls of the mould pour out surplus.

3 Allow the mould to drain by resting it, inverted, on two boards over a bowl or bucket.

4 Fettle (trim) off unwanted deposits of slip from the face of the mould with a steel palette.

You will need:
Casting slip
Plaster mould
Bowl
2 boards
Scraper
Plaster
Fine abrasive paper

A further application of plaster moulds in pot making is in the slip casting technique. Slip is a fluid consisting of a suspension of clay particles in water. In the casting technique plaster moulds are filled with a carefully prepared slip and allowed to stand full for a short length of time. During this period the plaster absorbs water from the slip and a layer of clay is deposited on the walls of the mould. The surplus slip may then be poured off and the cast within the mould allowed to stiffen and later removed.

Casting has the advantages of allowing quick and easy repetition of forms and also allows pots of extreme thinness, delicacy and precision of surface to be made.

The mould
Do not be too ambitious over the scale of your first slip-cast piece. Plan to make a reasonably small

5 Pour or splash trajectories of slip onto the surface of a plaster slab to form a lace-like structure.

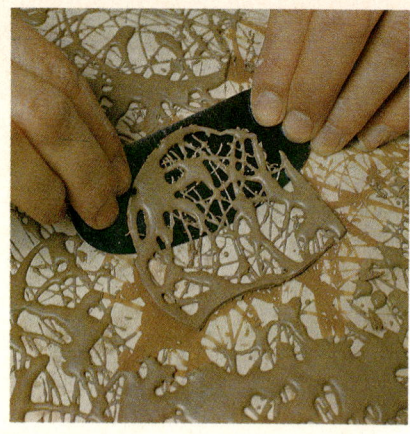

6 Separate selected areas of 'lace' from the mass and carefully lift them free from the plaster.

7 Join 'lace' to the parent form with slip to produce a low relief or free-standing motif.

object and graduate to larger and more complex pieces after you have mastered the process.

You can make up your casting mould from a clay model, as for the dish mould (page 16), or you can attach a piece of leather-hard clay to the head of a potter's wheel (using a little slip as an adhesive) and, using the wheel like a lathe, turn a suitable model with the assitance of trimming tools. A third alternative is to cast part of an attractive natural object, such as half a large green pepper or part of a fruit. The only points to remember in this respect are that since we are making only a one piece mould the cast will not free itself from the mould if it is prevented from doing so by undercutting and, secondly, the model for the mould must either be flexible or of such a material as will allow it to be easily cut out of the plaster.

Use a superfine grade of plaster for your mould and make up your plaster as dense as possible.

'Lace' decoration transforms this slip cast pot from a simple, easily reproduced utensil to a unique object.

The slip
Casting slips are unlike an ordinary mixture of clay and water in two respects. Firstly, they are largely non-plastic and shrink little. Secondly, the water content of a casting slip is converted into a charged electrolyte by the addition of small amounts of substances termed deflocculants. This causes the charged clay particles to repel one another rather than stick together. The result is that a fluid slip can be made using a great deal less water than is usually the case, giving the benefit of less shrinkage, cracking and distortion.

Buy a ready prepared earthenware casting slip, mix it before use and pass it through a fine sieve to remove any lumps.

Casting
Make certain that the mould is clean and fairly dry. Paradoxically, if it has been allowed to dry out completely wipe over its interior surface with a clean, moist sponge.

If it is a new mould, never previously used, a 'waste filling' is recommended to remove plaster scum. Prior to filling the mould for the first cast, pour the slip slowly from one jug into another, alllowing it to flow gently down its inside surface, and repeat until no further air bubbles are seen.

Use a wide-necked jug to fill the mould. Pour in the slip evenly and not too quickly. Do not allow it to run down the sides of the mould and do not stop or hesitate in your pouring until the mould is full. Fill the mould so that a slight protuberance of slip can be seen above the face of the plaster. As the plaster begins to absorb the water the level of slip will fall. Top up with slip to the original level.

The time it takes for a satisfactory thickness of clay wall to develop depends upon the thickness desired, the absorbency of the mould and the amount of moisture it already contains. Try two minutes for your first attempt and thereafter adjust the time in the light of this experience to produce whatever thickness is required.

When you have achieved the required thickness of clay wall lift the mould carefully and pour the surplus slip out into a bowl (not back into the filling jug if other moulds are to be filled with that mix). Set two boards across the bowl, place the mould mouth downwards upon them and allow the slip to drain for two or three minutes before returning the mould to its normal position.

Trim off the surplus clay that has spilled across the face of the mould as soon as it is stiff.

If you wish to apply free-form 'clay lace' additions to your piece you should begin to prepare them as soon as the main mould has been filled. Wipe over a flat plaster slab with a clean, damp sponge and form your lace by splashing, pouring or trailing casting slip onto its surface. Prepare considerably more than you think you will need. After

Slip-cast lemons shown at various stages of their production. Most fruits can be cast in this way.

about 15 minutes the lace will have dried sufficiently to be lifted from the plaster, trimmed with a sharp knife and bent to shape. Join to the main form with casting slip and press the additions into good contact with the walls of the cast form while it is still moist within the mould.

Twenty to 30 minutes from the time the surplus slip was poured out from the mould is usually a sufficient length of time to leave the cast in the mould. Remove the cast by inversion. (If it is reluctant to leave the mould let it stand for a few more minutes, then jar the mould a few times with blows from the hand.)

You can either rub down imperfections, when the pot is dry or, much less risky, bisque fire it (see page 49) with its imperfections to a low temperature – 750-800°C (1382-1472°F), then rub down with fine abrasive paper.

Carved Forms

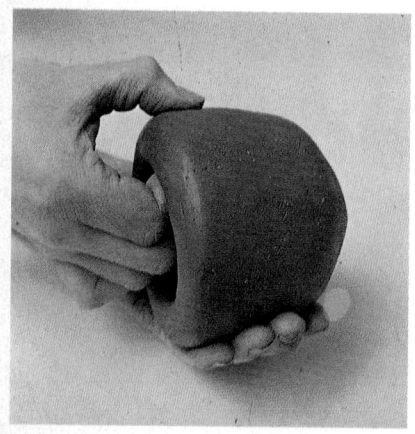

1 Raise a thick, domed form from a ball of clay by the pinching technique. Set it aside to stiffen.

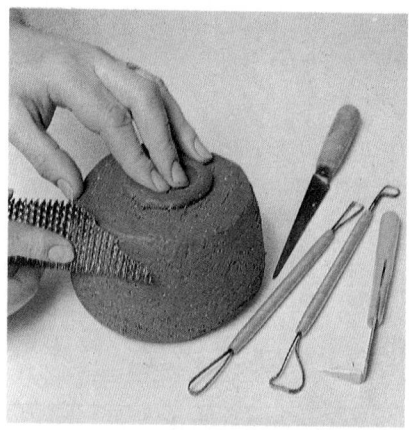

2 Cut the exterior base flat and carve a suitable foot-ring from the thick clay that remains.

3 Carve the exterior walls into the desired form, using knives, surform tools and gouges.

4 Carve interior of bowl to achieve walls of uniform thickness that relate to exterior profile.

You will need:
Clay with grog
Carving and surform tools
Knife or potter's pin
Potter's wire

The Japanese Raku Tea Ceremony bowls are the world's most aristocratic pottery wares produced by the carving process. It is a process which has great potential for creating new and exciting forms, since most of the modelling is carried out upon clay which is already stiff and self supporting. Many of the potter's fundamental disciplines and limitations that derive from the physical nature of soft clay are temporarily set aside to reveal a stimulating range of new skills and formal structures.

A good carving clay can easily be produced from any standard earthenware or stoneware body that has good plasticity simply by the addition of grog. The normal addition is about 35%. For general purposes use equal amounts of fine and medium grades. The inclusion of coarse grog, however, will give a marvellously natural, rock-like quality to the piece.

Carving pre-supposes that you start with a mass of material and that part of this mass is pared away. The clay carver has an advantage over the sculptor in marble, for example, in that his working material is malleable before it stiffens to a condition conducive to carving. During this stage the clay can be beaten and cut to the approximate size and shape of the intended form, thus saving a great deal of work at the carving stage. Carved pots are normally cut from a thick, generalized mass of clay raised to an approximation of the eventual hollow form by rudimentary pinching before being allowed to stiffen ready for carving. The box and bowl here show both techniques of working from a solid mass and from a basic, pinch-modelled form.

The process of actually carving the stiff clay can be done with any cutting tools, such as knives, gouges, planes and plaster working tools.

As can be seen from the photographs, there is a normal sequence of working when producing carved pottery. This involves completing the whole of the exterior form (except, perhaps, for some superficial details) before attempting to refine the interior beyond its most basic shape. It is normal to keep the interior of forms slightly moist with a lightly dampened cloth while the exterior is worked; the interior can then be cut back in relation to the exterior carving to give a uniformity of wall thickness throughout.

Forms should not be allowed to dry out completely until all work on them has been finished, since they become extremely fragile.

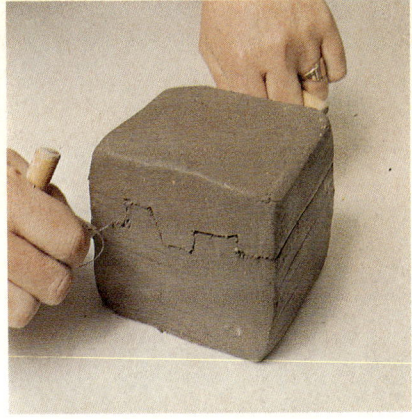

5 Use a wire to cut an interesting division into a block of fairly firm clay.

6 Hollow out the basic interior shapes of the two parts to form box and lid.

7 Carve the exterior into a sculptural form. You will need a variety of carving tools.

8 Refine the interior of the box so that it relates to your exterior modulations.

Precise control of the form coupled with a rugged and natural appearance are the features of carved wares.

Thrown Cylinder and Bottle

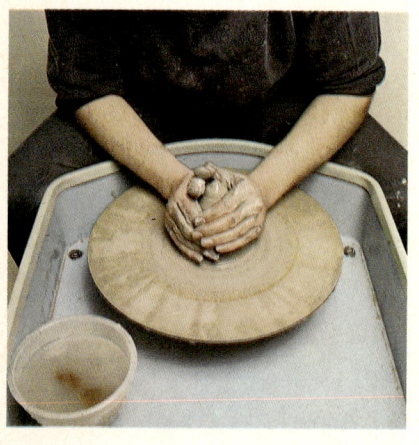

1 Place clay ball in centre of bat. Beat into cone. With wheel speed fast, lean on clay to centre.

2 Condition the clay to a circular forming process by pulling it up into an attenuated cone.

3 Force clay down into a centred disc with pressure from right hand. Control the shape formed with left.

4 Push left thumb down into centre of disc to leave a base some 12 mm ($\frac{1}{2}$ in.) thick.

5 Push left thumb horizontally across towards left palm to open up the flat interior base of cylinder.

6 Support pot wall from within. Eliminate any distortion in exterior of disc with gentle upward pressure.

You will need:
Moist, well kneaded clay
Small bowl of cold water
'Elephant ear' sponge
Potter's pin
Potter's knife
Potter's wire
Small strip of chamois leather

Throwing on the potter's wheel is the most common of all studio production techniques. It is particularly suited to the formation of symmetrical hollow ware, such as jars, bottles, flower containers, bowls, cups and teapots.

Most potters eventually develop an original throwing technique that suits them, which suggests that there is no one way to throw but many. The technique illustrated here is a good one for those learning to throw since it is relatively impersonal and therefore does not impede the later development of personal solutions. Also, it allows us to separate each stage of the process for individual consideration. Ultimately, of course, all these stages have to be fused together into a fluid process.

Throwing clay must be of good plasticity, moist and well kneaded. Divide your clay into neat balls about the size of an orange.

Potter's wheels come in many different designs. You stand to throw at some; at others you sit. They may be driven by electricity, constant foot treadle action or manual turning. Some have fixed plane metal heads; others are designed to carry 'throwing bats'. These bats are discs, usually of asbestos or plaster, which fix directly onto the wheel head and upon which the throwing is done. You can, if you wish, throw directly on the plane metal wheel heads or, alternatively and preferably, you can attach a plaster bat to them with a little slip.

7 To extrude walls upwards apply pressure to base of exterior. Support from within. Slowly pull hands up.

8 Repeat pull till pot is required height. Smooth rim with a piece of moist chamois leather.

9 Clean up exterior base of wall with a rib or cut in a finger grip with pin and knife. Cut free.

Smear the slip onto the metal head and centre the bat upon it. It will make a firm bond as the plaster absorbs the water from the slip.

Apply a little water to the clay and hands for the purpose of lubrication whenever necessary throughout the throwing process. Brace the arms against the knees or on the side of the wheel basin.

Do not be tempted to miss out on the stage of 'coning up' (**2**). This is vital to align the constituent lamellar particles of the clay mass.

The bottle form is simply a continuation of the cylinder.

Throw a cylinder of the required diameter and approximate height. Neck in its upper part with gently constricting pressure from both hands (**10**). As the diameter of the cylinder is reduced the thickness of the clay wall will increase. Ease this clay upwards with an additional pull to form the neck of the bottle.

Necking can also be used to correct flaring in cylinder forms.

Practice is vital for competent throwing. It is probably best not to try to produce pots at the first few sessions but rather to learn the process as thoroughly as possible.

10 Form narrow-necked bottles by constricting cylinder between two hands to reduce diameter. Re-pull.

Thrown Bowl

1 To throw bowl, cone and disc as for cylinder, making disc rather wider than for cylinder.

2 Open up curved interior base of bowl with pressure from fingers working from centre to rim.

3 Pull up walls to increase size of bowl and flare out to give the required curvature.

You will need:
Equipment listed on page 25

The thrown bowl is a seemingly simple form, but such satisfying simplicity is achieved only as a result of considerable aesthetic sensitivity.

The preliminary stages of centering, coning and forming the basic disc from which the pot is fashioned are identical for cylinder and bowl, except that a somewhat wider disc is normally made for bowls.

The first stage of the process is to throw the curved interior base of the bowl. Since this curve is the key to the whole form of the bowl it must be a carefully considered one. Wet the clay and hands and kick the wheel to a fast speed. With the fingers of the right hand held together, use the left hand to press them down into the centre of the clay before pulling them across in a sweeping, upward curving trajectory towards the right shoulder. As the fingers of the right hand move up and across the disc, allow the thumb of the right hand to move in unison up the exterior wall of the disc to restrain its tendency to flare outwards under pressure. The process may need to be repeated several times. Consolidate the lip after each pull.

The width of the bowl is most easily achieved by extruding the walls by the desired amount as a somewhat flaring cylinder, then modifying the curvature with a modelling pull. In this way sagging of the bowl is generally avoided.

Throwing is rather like ballroom dancing in that one partner leads and the other follows. In throwing the bowl the right hand, the initial leader, concedes leadership to the left midway through

4 Use a potter's pin to cut through the surplus clay at the base of the exterior wall.

5 Separate this clay from the bat with a horizontal knife cut and remove. Cut pot free with a wire.

the process.

The left hand begins from the centre of the bowl and moves up across the base, getting a sense of its curvature. The right hand applies pressure at the base of the disc and pulls the ridge of clay thereby formed gradually upwards in a near vertical line. When both hands arrive at the wall of the bowl the right one is slightly in the lead and the curving movement of the left forms a curved transition into the wall. The shoulder of the form being passed, the left hand accelerates ahead of the right into the cylinder throwing position and the remainder of the wall is formed in this way as a flaring cylinder.

Once the desired height of the wall has been formed a regular overall curvature of the bowl has to be achieved. This is done with one or two modelling pulls. The assessment and execution of this task lies with the left hand. With the wheel speed medium to slow, the modelling hand begins its work from the centre of the bowl, first assessing the basal curve, then extending it through into the side walls. The right hand supports the clay wall against the pressure from within the bowl and prevents general distortion.

Do not attempt to flare open a shallow bowl in one pull and slow the wheel speed with the increasing shallowness of the curvature.

Once the bowl form is complete remove some of the surplus clay from the base with the pin and knife (as for the cylinder) and cut through the clay with your potter's wire.

Remove the bat from the wheel and allow the bowl to stiffen before attempting to lift it free.

Trimming Thrown Forms

1 Centre the inverted leather-hard cylinder on the wheel. Use a finger to test centrality.

2 Attach pot to the wheel with a little plastic clay. Use a trimming tool to refine foot of side wall.

3 Carefully incise the foot-ring into the centre of the base of pot using a pointed tool.

4 Cut out the surplus clay from within the foot-ring to produce a recessed base.

You will need:
Selection of trimming tools
Small balls of plastic clay
Chamois leather
Chuck (for bottle)

The process of throwing on the potter's wheel produces pots which are thinly and evenly formed, except that in the majority of cases the foot is comparatively thick and unrefined. It can be trimmed to a more suitable profile when the pot has dried to a leather-hard condition.

Trimming or clay turning tools are used for this purpose. They come in a variety of designs and the selection of one type rather than another is largely a matter of availability and personal preference.

Trimming the cylinder
Assess the form of the leather-hard cylinder so that you know how much clay to remove and from what areas of the form.

Fix a clean throwing bat on your potter's wheel, invert your cylinder and place it, as nearly as you can, in the centre of the bat. Revolve the wheel slowly, holding a finger (or some other pointer) up against the lowest (i.e., nearest to

5 Cut away surplus clay surrounding the foot. Continue the line of the walls into the foot form.

6 Recess base to relate to the curved interior of the bowl. Finish foot with a moist chamois leather.

the bat with the pot in its present position) part of the form that requires trimming. The pot should revolve without gaps appearing between walls and marker. When the cylinder is centred secure it to the bat with three small balls of plastic clay. Use your trimming tool as illustrated to refine the base areas of the pot in the following stages.

Trim the unrefined exterior part of the pot.

Flatten the foot with a number of slow horizontal cuts.

Mark the position of the intended foot-ring with a pointed tool.

Recess the area contained within the foot-ring. This should be flat, relating to the flat interior of the cylinder. The clay left should be about the same thickness as the walls of the pot.

Shape the profile of the foot – a slightly rounded profile gives the pot more stability.

Smooth the surface of the foot-ring with a damp piece of chamois leather.

Trimming the bowl
The basic processes involved in trimming the cylinder are also applicable to the bowl, except that you must protect the bowl's lip. A number of methods are used to facilitate this. Some potters throw up a dome of plastic clay on the wheel to support the inverted bowl; others cover the face of the wheel or bat with a thin, flat slab of plastic clay. The bowl can be centred on this slab and held with three small balls of plastic clay.

Follow the steps described above for the cylinder. Take particular care, however, to make the shape of the foot grow naturally out of the form of the bowl. The area within the foot-ring should be curved both to follow the general line which runs through the bowl and to relate the exterior to the interior of the form.

Trimming the bottle
Trimming the bottle presents no new or special problems, except that the neck is too narrow and too fragile to support the pot in an inverted position. You need to use a chuck, which consists of a collar of clay attached to the wheel head in which the bottle is stood. Chucks may be thrown up from plastic clay when needed, or an alternative and more common method is to make a number of chucks of various shapes and sizes, bisque fire them (see page 49) and keep them for use when the need arises.

Soak the chuck in water and centre and attach it to the wheel bat exactly as if it were a pot to be trimmed. To protect the surface of the bottle and to provide a grip, line the mouth of the chuck with a thin strip of plastic clay.

Trim as previously described, remembering to relate the exterior form to the interior profile.

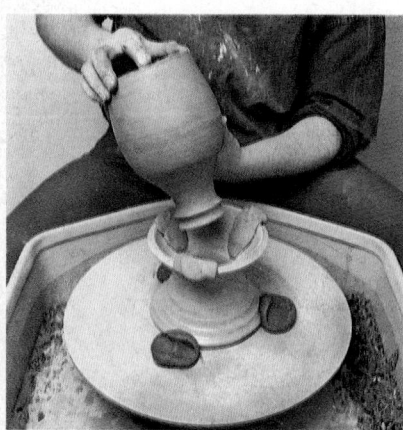

7 Trim the bottle within a prefired clay chuck. Line mouth with clay to grip and cushion pot.

8 Once the bottle is centred in the chuck trim the base by the standard technique for cylinder forms.

Composite Thrown Forms

You will need:
Equipment listed on page 25
Slip

A large variety of forms can be made by combining two or more thrown parts. In this project a simple conjunction of bowl and cylinder forms are used, in typical fashion, to produce a compote dish or goblets.

Most of the skills required for this project will have been learned during earlier ones but, since the key to a successful production of these forms is precision of working and foresight, it is useful as a means of developing your skills.

Bowl and cylinder forms are thrown separately and allowed to stiffen somewhat; the bowl is then trimmed to a suitable profile and the cylinder immediately attached to the inverted bowl while it is still in the trimming position. The cylinder is then re-thrown or modelled as necessary to produce a harmonious relationship with the bowl.

Since the centre of gravity is high in forms of this type, the design of the foot area is important if the piece is to have stability.

Use any standard throwing clay body for this project. Remember that the surface of the goblets will come into contact with the lips when the pot is in use and a clay which gives a pleasant smoothness of surface is to be preferred.

Throw the bowl element in the normal manner, as described on page 27. Since it will not need a foot-ring, it is not necessary to leave as much clay as usual at the base of the form.

The cylinder element may be thrown as it will be used or inverted, whichever is more practical for the design of form being attempted.

1 Throw up the two component parts: a bowl form and a stem (a variation on the cylinder).

2 Trim the bowl element to have a rounded base and an even thickness of wall throughout.

3 Score the base of the bowl where it is to receive the stem and the seat of the stem itself. Apply slip.

4 Use a tool or finger-tip to ensure the two elements are securely welded at point of contact.

5 Throw any necessary modifications into the stem. Smooth with a moist chamois leather or fingers.

Allow both elements to stiffen in the damp cupboard (see page 48). In this respect some forethought must be given to the amount of modelling which still needs to be done to the cylinder. If it has been thrown to what is virtually its final form both bowl and cylinder elements may be allowed to dry equally until in a soft leather state (do, however, cover the neck of the cylinder element with a small piece of damp cloth). If the cylinder still requires considerable modification cover it loosely with a piece of plastic sheeting so that it remains slightly more malleable than the bowl.

Trim the bowl to a domed base as shown. Measure the diameter of the cylinder neck and score the base of the bowl to receive it. Apply a liberal coating of slip to both contact surfaces before joining one to the other. Before you make too permanent a joint allow the wheel to revolve slowly and check that the cylinder is vertical. With the wheel revolving slowly, throw over the weld on the exterior and use a tool to weld over the join within the cylinder.

Re-throw or model the cylinder as necessary and cut off any excess at the foot with your potter's pin. Finally, smooth the foot of the form with a piece of moist chamois leather.

Return the composite piece to the damp cupboard for at least 24 hours to allow moisture to equalize. (If the cylinder element was much damper than the bowl at the time of joining wrap the piece in plastic sheeting for 24 hours and then allow another day at least in the damp cupboard.)

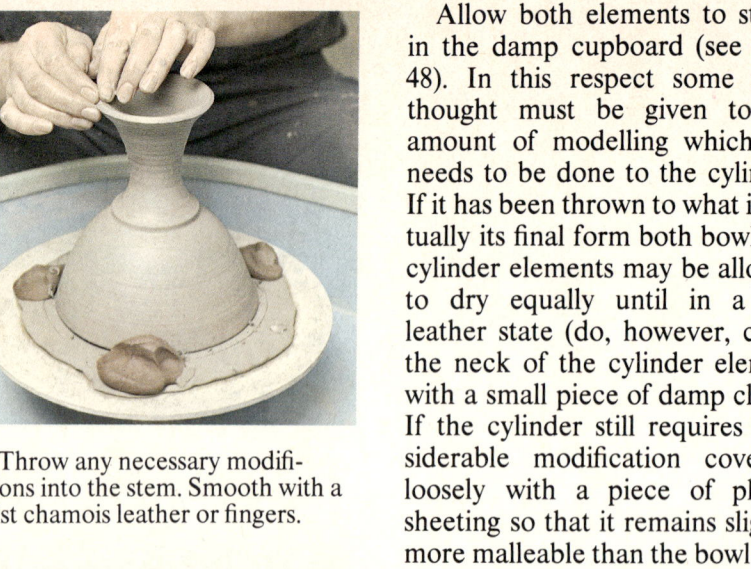

Hanging Planter

You will need:
Equipment listed on page 25
Cord

The planter consists of two parts, made in the same way.

Wedge 15% fine grog into a good plastic throwing body. Centre up a fairly large mass and, as for a bowl, form a rounded interior base, leaving a considerable thickness of clay beneath it.

Pull up the walls to form a convergent bowl form. If the clay is soft by this time let it sit in the open studio for an hour before flaring over the top 50mm (2in.) to form the rim. Allow to stiffen in the damp cupboard (see page 48) until leather-hard.

Using trimming tools, cut back the thick clay to produce a sculptural motif for the base of the pot and a pleasantly shaped lower form to the bowl. Drill down the centre to form a drainage hole.

Allow the moisture content of the piece to equalize in the damp cupboard, then cut 3 or 4 holes in the rim. Let dry slowly. The supporting cords pass through the central hole in the top, so make it large; rub down all sharp edges.

Fire the form to its maximum strength. No glaze is necessary.

1 Throw a large bowl form. Make walls rather higher than usual. Flare out rim and turn it over.

2 Trim away the thick clay from the base of the bowl to create a decorative motif.

3 Make the base relate well in visual terms to the bowl. Pierce a drainage hole into bowl.

4 Cut four holes through the rim to accept supporting cords. Make lid in same manner.

33

Jug and Teapot

1 Support the wall of the pot on either side of the point where the lip is to be pulled.

2 Use a stroking motion with fingers to pull the pouring lip. Smooth rim with a chamois leather.

You will need:
Equipment listed on page 25
Slip
Calipers

A great many pottery wares are made for use as containers or dispensers of liquid and, while the basic form of jugs or pitchers can be thrown as a variation on the cylinder technique previously described, they usually need lips or spouts added.

Lips
The pulled lip is the simplest pouring device to make and requires only a little deft manipulation to the thrown form. Some potters pull the lip directly after throwing; others prefer to pull the lips on a number of pieces after they have had an hour or so in which to lose their first wetness. In any case, it must be done while the clay is soft and very malleable.

Select the point on the rim of the pot where you wish to form the lip and support the adjacent areas of the wall on either side with the index and second fingers of the left hand. The lip is pulled forward between these supports by the right index finger (or two fingers if you require a wide lip).

Remember that the liquid has to flow smoothly from the main belly of the pot, so the lip needs to start from this area. Damp the index finger of the right hand with water and, with a number of firm but gentle upward stroking motions, gradually stretch the clay mouth of the pot into the lip required.

The actual pouring point needs to be quite thin if liquids are not to dribble back down the outside after pouring.

Finally, smooth the lip with a scrap of damp chamois leather.

Spouts
Spouts are simply thrown appendages that are joined onto larger forms with a little slip. They are easy to make, but inexperienced potters find difficulty in positioning a spout so that it functions well and still has the appearance of absolute harmony with the larger form.

Throw and trim the body of the pot, but keep it moist in the damp cupboard. Throw a number of small cylinder forms which you consider might be suitable as spouts and allow them to stiffen to a condition similar to that of the pot. Use a potter's knife to shape the base of the spout so that it relates to the area of the pot where it is to be joined.

Pierce the wall of the pot with the perforations that will feed liquid to the spout with a fine hole cutter, a small wood drill or the point of your knife.

Score all surfaces to be involved in the join with the potter's pin, apply a liberal coating of a slip made from the throwing clay in use and press the two parts together.

The spout may be shaped further, and other additions made to the base form, if required, then the pot should be returned to the damp cupboard to allow moisture to equalize.

Handles
The pulling of handles is an acquired skill and you must not expect instant results.

Start with a thick coil of the same clay as you used to throw the main body of the pot. Make certain it is moist and well kneaded.

Cut off a piece of the coil about 10cm (4in.) long and grasp it in the left hand.

Wet the right hand and extrude the handle between the fingers and the thumb by drawing the hand down the length of the coil. A dozen or more stroking actions may be required to do this. Lubricate the right hand after each pull.

Bend the extruded handles into suitable curves and allow them to stiffen on a board in the open air for an hour or so. Trim off the excess clay and attach the handles to previously scored areas of the pot surface with a little stiff slip.

Covers
Simple covers are the easiest of all lids to make – just a low trimmed cylinder form which fits inverted over the pot's neck.

Make the cover immediately

3 Throw a tapered cylinder suitable for a spout. Allow to stiffen before shaping to fit pot.

4 Score both surfaces with pin and pierce the grid. Apply slip before pressing spout into place.

5 To throw a cover, measure the exterior diameter of the neck to be fitted with calipers.

6 This measurement is the internal diameter of the cover which is thrown as a low cylinder.

after the main body of the pot. Use a pair of calipers to measure the exterior diameter of the neck and throw a low cylinder with the same internal diameter.

Allow the pot and cover to stiffen under the same conditions and trim them together.

Attach the cover form to the wheel in the normal manner for trimming cylinders and shape the unrefined base area into the profile required.

There should be an easy fit between pot and cover. If the cover is too tight trim a little clay from the interior wall.

7 Trim the top of the cover to the desired profile as for cylinder or bowl bases (see page 29).

35

 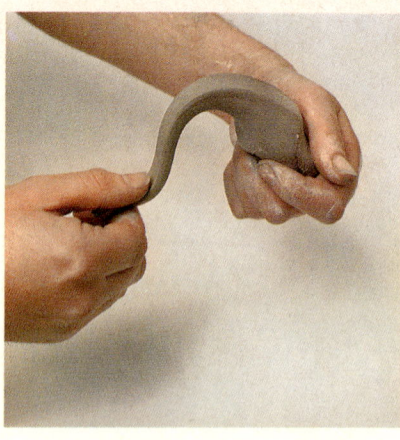 

8 Pull a handle from well kneaded clay. Grasp clay in the left hand and extrude with the right.

9 Keeping right hand wet, slowly pull out handle. Bend to shape and leave to stiffen on board.

10 Score and apply slip to surfaces to be joined. Weld the two parts firmly together.

Oxides

You will need:
Various oxides
Scales
Water
Slip
Glaze
Brushes
Organic material
Scraper

The simplest colouring agent in pottery is clay itself, either the natural colour of the clay from which the pot is made or surface dressing of slip derived from a clay which fires to a contrasting colour. In this way a whole range of natural colours consisting of black, browns, earth reds, greys, tans and white are obtained.

Pure clay is normally white and the variety of colours mentioned above result from the fact that the vast majority of clays are polluted by colourants which occur naturally in them in the form of metallic oxides.

The oxides of each metal produce a distinctive colour when used in ceramics although that colour does not always emerge until after glaze firing.

The production or separation of oxides by laboratory or industrial processes have added a wide range of chromatic hues to the potter's repertoire and today, by combining the oxides of various metals together, the potter can achieve virtually any colour he desires.

The word 'oxide' is used as a general term by potters. The material actually used may well be a simple oxide, but it might equally be a carbonate, a dioxide or a pentoxide and still be termed 'oxide'.

Oxides are the most common colourants for glazes and, although some (such as iron and

1 To mix oxides, make a thin, paint-like consistency with oxide, water and slip or glaze.

2 The colour effects of oxides in a glaze can be tested by painting onto the surface of a glazed tile.

3 When this tile is re-fired the oxides burn into the glaze and take on their characteristic colours.

manganese) may be used to colour clay or clay slip, ceramic stains derived from oxides are normally preferred for this purpose. Oxides and stains may also be used in a relatively concentrated form as a medium for brushwork and other decorative techniques (see pages 42-45).

The oxides of each metal differ from element to element in their tinting strength and in the percentages that need to be added to a glaze to produce a given strength of colour.

A list of the colours obtained when firing wares in an electric kiln, using the more popular oxides, is given here on the table on the right together with the percentage additions required to produce workable colours.

Single oxides used alone sometimes produce glazes that are garish in colour. Consequently, many potters prefer to mute these colourants with a second oxide. Iron oxide is very commonly used in this way and two typical examples are given below.

Muted green
Copper carbonate 3%
Red iron oxide 1%

Muted blue
Cobalt carbonate 1%
Red iron oxide 1%

Nickle oxide (½-1%) and manganese dioxide (1%) are also popular additions for this purpose and may replace the iron oxide in the above examples and other similar cases.

Black is normally achieved in glazes by using a combination of oxides – a useful one is that given below.

Red iron oxide 8%
Manganese dioxide 3%
Cobalt oxide 1%

Material	Colour produced	% addition to glaze	% addition to slip
Tin oxide	pure white	5	–
Nickel oxide	grey-green	1-2	
Iron chromate	grey	2	2
Red iron oxide	red-brown	4-6	3-4
Red iron oxide	tan	2	2
Copper oxide	green	2	
Copper carbonate	green	3-4	
Cobalt oxide	blue	$\frac{1}{4}-\frac{1}{2}$	
Cobalt carbonate	blue	$\frac{1}{2}-1\frac{1}{2}$	
Manganese dioxide	brown	2-4	2
Manganese carbonate	plum	5	
Depleted uranium oxide	yellow	2-7	
Zirconium oxide (or zirconium silicate)	hard white	6-12	
Chromium oxide	green	1-3	
Rutile (impure titanium)	cream-tan	3-5	

4 Incised or impressed motifs may be stained with a mixture of oxide and slip for colour contrast.

5 Remove surplus oxide from surrounding areas by scraping lightly with a steel palette.

Industrially prepared stains are preferred to oxides for the production of certain colours. Stains are particularly popular for colouring clays and slips. Some stains can be used in either clays or glazes but others are suitable for use in only one of these two materials. If in doubt, consult the catalogue of your ceramics supplier for precise details of colours available, applicability and percentage additions.

Stains are the most common glaze colourants in the following cases.

Bright red:
Cadmium-Selenium stain 3-5%

Yellow
Vanadium stain
(Tin-vanadium stain) 4-6%
or *Praeodymium yellow stain* 5%

Colouring a clay or glaze slip with oxide or stain
First, calculate the weight of the oxide or stain against the dry weight of the clay or glaze you plan to use to make up the slip.

It is very important to calculate the amount of oxide you use precisely. Even so, circumstances affect your results considerably, and it is as well to remember that a moist clay that does not absorb water gives a thinner result than a more porous one.

Either thoroughly disperse the dry colourant through the dry powder before slaking or, alternatively, mix the oxide or stain with a little water and pass it through a very fine sieve. The sieved material can be added to fluid slip which should first be thoroughly mixed and sieved.

Making up an oxide mixture for decorating unfired clay
Mix a level teaspoonful of the appropriate oxide (less of the strong oxides of copper and cobalt) with half a cup of water. Add two teaspoons of white slip and mix thoroughly. The resulting fluid is an ideal painting medium for applying brushwork decoration to clay that has dried to a leather-hard condition. See page 42 for some suggestions for decorative ways of applying this mixture.

Making up an oxide mixture for decorating on top of an unfired glaze film
Mix a level teaspoonful of oxide (less of copper or cobalt oxides) with half a cup of water. Add two teaspoons of the glaze already used on the piece and mix thoroughly.

Apply the brushwork decoration carefully to the pot as soon after it has been glazed as is practicable.

If you know in advance that you will be applying decoration on top of the glaze surface you will find it advantageous to add a little glaze gum to your glaze slip prior to use. This will strengthen the underlying glaze film and make it more resilient to pressure from the decorating brush.

A transparent glaze softens the line of oxide brushwork when the pot is fired.

6 Natural objects, such as a leaf or grasses, can be used as a mask against background applications of oxide.

7 One of the most common uses of oxides is as glaze colourants. Percentage additions must be precise.

Surface Decoration

1   Fill a low relief mould with clay, scrape off the surplus and pull the sprig free when stiff.

2   Score both surfaces with a potter's pin and apply a coat of slip. Press the sprig into place.

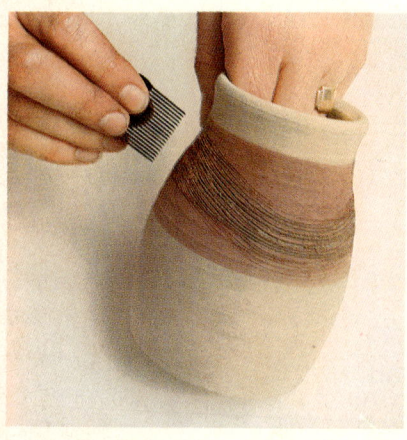

3   Decorative motifs may be combed into leather-hard clay. Comb through a layer of slip for colour contrast.

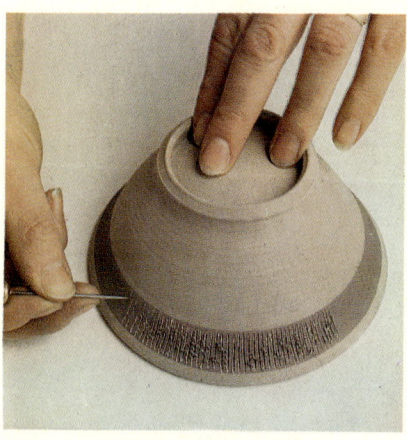

4   Sgraffito is a linear decoration incised into leather-hard clay with a pointed tool.

You will need:
Comb
Slip
Wooden paddle
Organic material
Textured surfaces
Moulds
Cast or carved plaster shapes

Surface decoration of the raw pot may take several forms, but they fall into the two general categories: articulated surfaces that are the natural result of the forming process and decoration that is added as embellishment to the completed form.

Coil pottery which has not been paddled or scraped down is a good example of the first category.

Combing can also be used in this same manner to impart an overall texture to hand built forms. A random pattern is normally more effective than an attempt to use the comb for regular or fine fluting effects.

A short length of comb can also be used to produce a vigorous, individual incised motif into pottery. This must be executed with verve to be successful. The application of a coat of slip (of a colour which contrasts with the

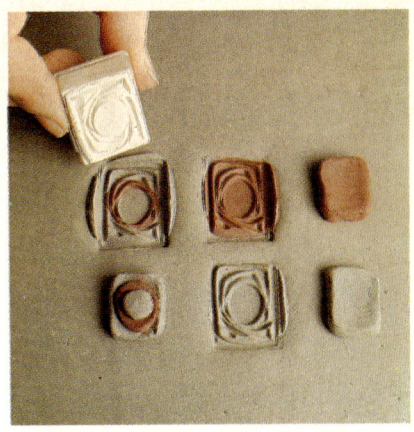
5 Carved wood or plaster stamps can be effectively used to raise low relief devices on pot walls.

6 Clay is conducive to being textured in a distinctive way by almost any tool or object.

7 Natural matter can be pressed into clay and left to burn out during firing.

clay body) prior to combing increases the visual effect, since the comb cuts through to the underlying body, thus creating a two-tone effect.

The marks left in pottery surfaces by paddling can in themselves be exciting. Their decorative qualities can be further enhanced by carving decorative motifs into the surface of your paddles. This will be transferred to the clay wall as low relief and can be extremely effective.

Another popular form of surface enrichment can be achieved by beating organic material into the exterior walls of pottery with a paddle. This burns away during the bisque firing to leave a relief impression in the clay. Rice, straw and grasses are the substances most commonly used for this purpose.

Inherent textural decoration may be achieved in slab pottery by rolling out the clay slabs on distinctively textured surfaces such as weathered wooden boards, oriental straw matting or coarse jute sacking rather than the usual, featureless, close-woven canvas or cloth.

Intaglio decorative motifs that are more obviously applied embellishments may be made by pressing any hard object into the clay surface and removing it to leave an impression. Individual pressings of this type are difficult to make work well but can be effective when used as a frieze running around a form or when a variety of impressions are used together to form a larger, confident motif.

Running frieze patterns (intaglio or low relief) can also be effectively achieved using a simple carved plaster roller. The frieze may be rolled directly into the clay wall or a strip of soft clay may be joined to the wall with slip which, when it is rolled, leaves a raised frieze in its wake.

Relief medallions to be luted or sprigged onto the walls of pots may also be made from cast or carved plaster shapes. The shape is carved, as shown, and the medallion formed by pressing the plaster stamp onto a ball of soft clay. Join the medallion to the leather-hard pot with slip.

Sprig motif (above right) echoes floral shapes. A basic thrown form (right) by Ian Godfrey is embellished with applied motifs.

Slip Decoration

1 The colour or surface of clay wares can be changed or modified by a 'dressing' of slip.

2 Motifs in slip can be drawn with a slip trailer. Train onto a soft dressing for best results.

3 For brushwork decoration select a brush which makes a mark appropriate to the spirit of the design.

You will need:
Various slips
Sieve
Brushes
Potter's pin
Banding wheel
Slip trailer
Feather
Wax
Newspaper

Slip is one of the cheapest and most popular decorative materials used in pottery. At its simplest it is a clay or clay body which has been mixed with water and sieved to form an homogenous fluid. Use a coarse sieve to disperse clay lumps when first preparing the slip, but you may well have to use a finer sieve subsequently. Always mix and sieve the slip immediately before use and adjust its consistency to that required by the technique to be employed. (Slip may be thinned simply by blending in additional water. Excess water can be siphoned off from slip after it has settled.)

Always keep your slip in a covered container and do not allow splashes of it to dry on the sides.

Marbling
Decorating the interior surfaces of moulded dishes with a marbled slip pattern is easy to do and can produce very professional results under a transparent glaze.

Form your dish within the press mould as normal, trim its lip and allow it to stand in the air for an hour or so until its surface has stiffened a little. Prepare and sieve two slips of differing colours. Both should be of moderate thickness so that they retain their autonomy during marbling; on the other hand the slip must be sufficiently fluid to

4 For marbling, press the interior of the dish with a film of slip and pour off the surplus.

5 Add contrasting slips and manipulate the dish so that the fluids flow to leave marbled pattern.

6 Cut or tear pieces of absorbent paper to act as masks and press onto moist clay. Paint over.

7 When the applied slip has stiffened lift the edges of paper with a pin and pull free to leave design.

8 Further masks may be applied and other colours of slip used to create a polychrome design.

flow easily.

Pour the lighter coloured of the two slips into the dish (still supported within the mould) and tilt it so that the slip swills around within the form until all the surface has been dressed. Pour out most of the excess slip which has not been used up in this process by tipping the mould up into a near vertical position (**4**).

Pour some small amounts of the second slip onto the wet dressing. Distribute these additions about the bowl rather than adding all the darker slip in one place. Tilt and roll the mould so that the fluid slips sweep and flow about the form. A marbled pattern of the two colours will gradually develop (**5**).

When you are happy with the effect achieved tip the mould again into the near vertical position and allow the excess slips to run out of the dish. Wipe the edge of the dish with your potter's sponge, allow it to stiffen and remove it from the mould by the normal inversion method when it is leather-hard.

Cut paper masks

Cut or torn paper masks may be applied to the surface of a pottery form, either beneath dressings of slip or between layers of glaze, to produce effects technically similar to wax resist.

Paper mask decoration may be used on any pottery form, but it is most successful on moulded dishes.

Cut or tear suitable paper shapes from any kind of thin absorbent paper (newspaper is ideal) and press them down onto the surface of the moulded dish soon after it is made so that they stick to its surface (**6**).

The bowl may be dressed with a contrasting coloured slip or painted or sprayed over with a thin mixture of slip and metallic oxide. Allow the dressing to become semi-stiff before lifting a corner of each piece of paper mask with your potter's pin. Carefully lift each piece of paper free, bringing its covering of slip with it to reveal the complete two-colour effect (**7** and **8**).

Painted decoration

Painted brushwork decoration using slip as a medium is one of the most illustrious of all forms of pottery decoration.

Pointed Japanese calligraphic brushes called *fude* are the best

43

9 Some shapes are enhanced by the addition of bands of slip (or oxides) applied on a banding wheel.

10 For feathered decoration, trail slip onto a fresh dressing of contrasting coloured slip.

11 Draw a feather or fine brush across the slip trailing to produce the typical pattern.

ones to use, but experiment with a variety of types including some you make yourself from bundles of straw and grasses.

Brushwork can use slip of a colour which contrasts with the clay body colour as its medium or slip coloured with metallic oxides (see page 39) or, indeed, suspensions of metallic oxides in water alone.

It is difficult to give a guide to the best consistency for brushing slip, except to say that it should be reasonably thin and creamy. Test it out on some scrap clay until you arrive at a consistency which suits you. Pass the slip through a fine sieve to disperse any lumps and mix thoroughly prior to use. Apply the slip quickly, surely and confidently.

The oriental slip decoration known as *hakeme* consists of a brief and vigorous application of slip applied with a broad homemade brush of dried grasses. When done well it is impressive under a transparent glaze.

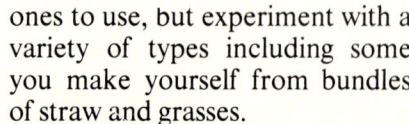

White slip vigorously applied with a homemade grass brush and covered with a transparent glaze (Hakeme).

12 Paint patterns onto the walls of leather-hard forms with colourless liquefied wax.

13 Apply slip or oxide. The wax acts as a resist and a two-colour pattern emerges.

Splashing and whirling

Dramatic decorative effects can be achieved by splashing slip onto a pottery form.

Slip for splashed decoration should be of rather thicker consistency than for brushwork if runs are to be avoided.

Whirling, like splashing, is a dramatic random technique. It is normally used to decorate plates and shallow dishes or bowls.

Attach the leather-hard plate, face uppermost, to your potter's wheel or a heavy banding wheel with some soft clay. (Moulded dishes may be decorated in this way while still contained within the mould). Spin the wheel at a fairly brisk pace and spill some thin slip onto the centre of the revolving plate from a jug or plastic cup. Centrifugal force will throw the slip out towards the circumference to produce a strong decorative device. It is normal to apply two or more coloured slips in this way.

The consistency of slip for whirled decoration needs to be quite thin if a kinetic effect is to be achieved.

Trailing

The trailing of slip onto pottery wares from a narrow-necked reservoir to produce an active linear design has been popular for centuries.

Slip for trailing needs to be evenly mixed and should be passed through a fine sieve prior to use. It must not be too thin.

The most common form of slip trailer consists of a rubber bulb with a detachable nozzle which allows for easy charging with slip and cleaning.

The slip may be trailed directly onto the semi-stiff clay form but, since this produces decoration with an exaggerated profile, it is preferable to apply a coat of slip (dressing) to the entire surface to be decorated. The decoration is then drawn onto this moist film so that some degree of integration between the two slips is possible (**10**).

A variation on the slip trailing techniques is feathering. Apply alternate trails of different coloured slips to the clay surface and produce the typical pattern by drawing a fine feather across the bands while the slip is still wet (**11**).

Wax resist

Wax resists and repels water, a fact that allows wax to be used as an effective and simple decorative masking agent against such aqueous solutions as clay slips, glazes and suspensions of metallic oxides in water.

Break up some pieces of white paraffin wax (candle wax), place them in an old saucepan, shallow pan or double boiler and warm over a low heat until just liquefied. Remove the pan from the heat and add thin machine oil – up to about half the volume of wax – and warm the mixture gently, mixing until smooth. The wax solidifies again upon cooling.

The wax may be painted (once a brush has been used for wax keep it for this purpose alone), splashed or dripped onto the surface of any clay form, where it solidifies and thereby masks the application of any aqueous solution (**12**).

Dip the pot into thin slip or paint slip or metallic oxide solution over all or part of the clay form. These materials will adhere to the bare clay, but will be rejected by the wax. The wax burns away in the kiln during firing to leave a two-colour decoration (**13**).

After bisque firing wax resist may be used under or between layers of glaze to produce two-colour glaze effects.

Inlaid Decoration

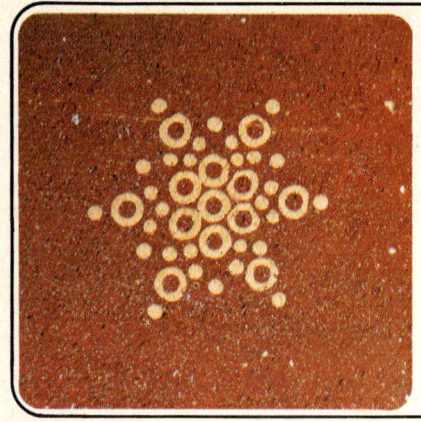

1 Paint the motif onto the form with slip. Cut the pattern into the surface with a fine gouge.

2 Alternatively, motifs may be impressed into the clay using carved stamps or simple punches.

3 Pack incisions with stiff slip. Take care to fill the depth of cut. Work along incised lines.

4 When inlay has stiffened remove surplus with scraper or knife to reveal two-colour motif.

You will need:
Stiff slip or plastic clay
Gouges
Cut, carved or cast stamps
Slip and brush (for painting)
Small palette knife
Plastic sheeting
Scrapers

The practice of inlaying materials of contrasting colour into the surfaces of artifacts for decorative effect is common in many of the crafts.

The inlay process as used by the potter is oriental in origin and is properly termed 'mishima'.

Pottery inlay consists of cutting decorative patterns into the surface of leather-hard clay forms or pressing decorative motifs into the clay while it is still semi-plastic. These negative cuts or impressions are then packed with stiff slip or plastic clay of contrasting colour, which is allowed to stiffen. Finally, the excess filling material is scraped off to reveal a clearly defined, coloured motif within the clay surface, which will eventually be allowed to show through a transparent glaze.

Mishima decoration is usually of a linear character, but larger areas can be inlaid if required.

Cutting tools for mishima should be sharp. They should also be of the gouge type, which actually removes a ribbon of clay rather than simply raising a burr on each side of the incision. Linocutting gouges are ideal. Stamps for impressed mishima may be cut from wood, carved from cast plaster blanks or from fine clay and bisque fired before use.

Impress the stamps into the clay when it has stiffened somewhat after forming, but is still less than hard. Support the wall against the pressure from the stamp, otherwise distortions or cracks will develop. Try and push the stamp straight into the clay rather than working it in gradually with a rocking motion.

When cutting motifs into clay walls you need the pot to be in a rigid, leather-hard condition. Some potters like to paint the design they plan to cut onto the pot's surface with slip as a guide before actual cutting begins. You will find that by varying the depth of your cut you can produce varying widths of line.

One of the most common faults is to cut too deeply into the form – about one quarter of the thickness of the wall is the normal maximum.

The filler may be quite simply a plastic clay of a different colour or a coloured slip. White slip may be coloured or the colour of lighter slips reinforced by the inclusion of some body stain or metallic oxide (see page 39). Avoid the more potent oxides such as cobalt and copper, however, since they tend to leave an unsightly blush around the inlaid motif.

The use of a transparent glaze accentuates the colour contrast between the clay and the inlay.

A fluid slip may be dried to a stiff consistency by pouring it onto a plaster slab or into a plaster mould for a short time.

Use a flexible metal tool, such as a small palette knife, to pack the filler into the incisions.

Start at one end and work along it rather than trying to fill it all at once or working from both ends. Leave the filler piled up a little above the pot surface.

Wrap the whole pot in plastic for about 24 hours.

Carefully shave, scrape or plane the excess filling material down until the motif appears. It is normally necessary to remove a fine film of the surrounding body before optimum clarity is obtained. The contrast between the two clays will in any case be increased after firing.

The idea suggested earlier (page 41) of pressing grains of rice into the walls of pots is very effective when used in conjunction with mishima. The glaze film builds up in these depressions left after the rice has burned away and provides a subtle new dimension to the decoration.

The Damp Cupboard and Drying

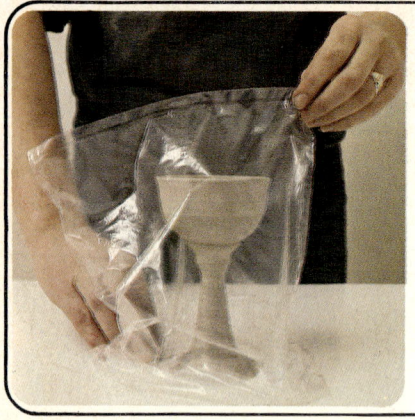

1 Damp cupboard walls must be non-porous. Plaster shelves are ideal: keep then saturated.

2 You can improvise with a slab of water-saturated plaster, props and plastic sheeting.

You will need:
Plastic sheeting
Damp cupboard or box
Strips of damp cloth

Proper drying is vital to the production of pottery wares. Imperfect drying technique is responsible for many of the problems encountered by the hobbyist and student potter.

There are three drying phases which the potter has to control.

Equalization of moisture
Whenever additions are luted or otherwise joined onto a pot to form a composite piece the moisture content throughout the whole must be equalized before proceeding to drying. Enclose the whole piece in plastic sheeting for a minimum of 24 hours (longer for larger wares).

Stiffening
The next stage is a very slow process of stiffening. This is done inside a damp cupboard or damp box.

The cupboard or box must have a close-fitting door and its interior surface sealed with an impermeable material such as zinc cladding, fibreglass or heavy plastic sheeting.

The atmosphere within must be kept humid, either with a humidifier or with saturated plaster of Paris bats.

Pots will need to be kept in the damp cupboard for about a week.

Thin appendages on pots (such as spouts and handles) tend to dry out faster than the main body of the pot. To prevent fracture wrap these elements with strips of damp cloth.

Drying
Once the pots have stiffened they can be brought out into the open air.

Drying shelves should be made of slats of wood or expanded metal so that air can reach all parts of the drying form. Hollow ware is best dried standing on its lip.

Test the ware for dryness against the cheek or inner arm; a cold, clammy feeling indicates the presence of more moisture than in the general atmosphere.

Do not bisque fire wares until they are totally dry. This may take several weeks for thick forms.

Dry, unfired pottery is very fragile and must be handled with great care.

Packing and Firing the Kiln

1 Check that kiln shelves are sound. Paint upper surface with bat-wash; clean edges and underside.

2 Support each shelf on three refractory props of suitable height. Low ones support effective floor.

3 Bisque fire pots with lids in place and bowls prone to distortion on their lips.

You will need:
Bat wash
Selection of kiln furniture
Pyrometric cones
Pyrometer and thermocouple

The bisque firing
When pots are completely dry they are ready for the first firing, the bisque (or biscuit) firing. This produces a chemical change in the clay, converting it irreversibly into a hard, rock-like material. Read all the general information on kilns and firing in this chapter before you embark on this process.

Wares may touch one another during this firing so put small forms in larger ones and stack sets of pieces in a lip to lip, foot to foot system, known as 'bungs'. Pots with lids should be fired with the lid in place. Aim for an equal density of pack throughout the kiln.

Fire large bowls standing on their lips and small bowls in bungs to avoid warping. Fire geometric slab pots in the centre of the kiln.

Space kiln shelves evenly and use a three point support system (**2**). Keep pots and kiln shelves away from the electric elements.

If you are using pyrometric cones make certain that you can see them through the kiln peephole when the door is closed.

Firing schedule
There are a number of possible temperatures for bisque firing, but in the vast majority of cases stonewares and earthenwares can be bisque fired together to about 890-900°C (1634-1652°F).
Stage 1 – 0–200°C (32–392°F) – The pots contain considerable atmospheric moisture which needs to be dried out very slowly. Leave all the kiln peepholes and vents open and start the firing by leaving

the kiln on very low overnight. After 200°C (392°F) all physically held water is released. If this stage is rushed pots made of dense clay bodies will shatter. Beyond 200°C (392°F) the rate of temperature rise may be increased somewhat.

Stage 2 – 350-700°C (662-1292°F) – Continue to allow temperature to rise at only a modest rate since chemical bonded water is released from the clay molecule now. In fact, most water will have gone by 500°C (932°F), but for chemical reasons it is best not to increase the rate of temperature rise again before 580°C (1044°F). After 500°C (932°F) close any larger vents but leave door peepholes open.

Stage 3 – Up to 900°C (1652°F) – Organic matter burns out of the clay, carbon is released and inorganic materials convert to an oxidized form.

Allow the kiln to cool slowly and naturally. Do not attempt to open until 200°C (392°F).

Do not handle the wares unnecessarily when unpacking the kiln. It is best to wear gloves.

If the bisque fired wares are not to be glazed for some time, pack them in cardboard boxes or wrap in newspaper.

THE ELECTRIC KILN

This is normally a heavy gauge metal case lined with refractory fire bricks capable of withstanding high temperatures.

Kilns can be heated by fire from wood, gas or oil but electricity is the most widely used fuel. The interior walls of the electric kiln support coiled kanthal wire elements; some kilns also have elements in the door and floor. Most kilns are front- or top- loading.

Kiln elements can easily be damaged by burning if fragments of clay or glaze fall on them. Use a light brush or a vacuum cleaning device to remove foreign matter from the kiln before every firing. Handle the elements as little as possible.

SHELVING

The wares to be fired are stacked in the kiln on shelves; sometimes these shelves are made of refractory clay but more commonly of sillimanite. They are supported on refractory props.

Never fire wares directly on the kiln floor. Raise an effective floor of shelves about 12mm ($\frac{1}{2}$in.) above the floor on props. All the props used to carry subsequent shelves must be located vertically above these first ones. Use a three point system with two props at the mouth of the kiln and one prop at the centre back of the shelf. Reverse this pattern for the back shelf of kilns two shelves deep. Do not use cracked shelves (check by tapping) or warped ones.

Shelves are easily damaged by glaze which fuses on them to form glass. Protect them with a layer of bat wash (also called kiln wash) which can be bought from a ceramic supplier or made from 50% kaolin plus 50% flint mixed to a creamy consistency with water. Paint two or three coats on the top surfaces of the shelves only, cleaning up the sides if it runs down. If you are using old shelves chip off any droplets of glaze attached to the bat wash and fill in the dents with more wash. Never invert shelves once they have been coated. Brush down the backs before use.

Kilns fire more evenly if the load is of approximately equal density throughout.

Temperature

An accurate means of assessing temperatures within the kiln is essential. The first, and best, method is to use pyrometric

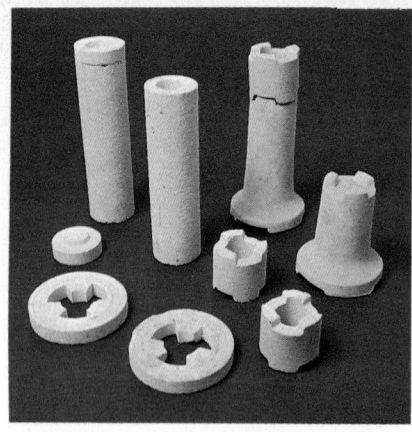

4 Refractory props are available in various designs to suit special needs and personal preferences.

5 Typical plaques of pyrometric cones showing correct angle of displacement from the vertical.

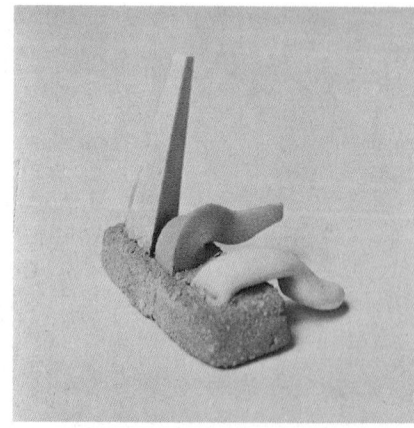

6 The cones bend in response to heat allowing you to check firing development.

7 Pyrometer and thermocouple enable you to assess the temperature inside the kiln with accuracy.

8 Typical kiln controls include fuses, warning lights and variable energy controller.

9 Partly unpacked kiln after typical glaze firing showing appearance of wares.

cones, compacted sticks of mixed ceramic materials with a known melting point. You can buy a range of them, covering the full temperature range. Each cone is coded to indicate its temperature equivalent. Cones are placed among the wares in a position where they can be observed through the peephole. By watching for their softening you can see when a given temperature has been reached.

First ascertain the temperature you require – select the appropriate cone with its higher and lower neighbours in the series. (There are international variations in notation systems.) Stand the three cones in sequence in a cone plaque or press them into a small slab of refractory clay (50% fireclay plus 50% grog) at an angle of about 8° from the vertical (see **5**). The centre cone indicates the required temperature. When the kiln approaches maturation temperature you will see the softer cone soften and slowly slump – the rise in kiln temperature should then be slowed. Precise temperatures are indicated at 45° and the required temperature is reached when the middle cone slumps to this angle.

If the third cone slumps overfiring has taken place – information which may be valuable later in diagnosing faults. The kiln may now be switched off or switched over to soak.

The other temperature measuring device is a pyrometer and thermocouple (**7**). The thermocouple is a silica sheath projecting through the kiln wall into the kiln chamber. It contains a bi-metal strip, whose constituent metals have a differing degree of reaction to heat. The pyrometer, which is simply a potentiometer, measures this reaction and translates it into an indication of temperature.

The pyrometer alone is satisfactory for bisque firing but a combination of cones and pyrometer is best for glaze firing.

The controls on electric kilns vary according to model. All are connected to a main power on/off switch – the kiln should never be opened when the switch is on. Most kilns have variable energy controls (0-100% activity) for each electrical phase and a device, most commonly worked through the pyrometer, which causes the kiln to switch off automatically when a pre-set temperature is reached. It is normally also possible for the maturation temperature simply to be maintained when it is reached; this condition is termed 'soaking' and is advantageous when glaze firing.

Some kilns have sophisticated systems of time clocks which allow the operator to prescribe a complete programme of requirements for implementation during the firing cycle which will then be effected automatically.

In addition, you should have some safety devices on your kiln. It is advisable to have it fitted with a switch which automatically cuts the current flow if the door is opened. The kiln door should also be lockable so that it cannot be opened during a firing. Finally, for the protection of the kiln, a heat fuse which cuts the flow of current should it be inadvertently fired to the limits of its capability is a worthwhile investment.

Glazes and Glost Firing

1 Pass the dry glaze through a sieve to break down lumps prior to slaking.

2 Mix the sieved, dry glaze with water in a bucket. Disperse all lumps for a smooth, creamy fluid.

You will need:
Various glazes
Sieves
Water
Buckets and jugs
Brush
Wooden boards

Some types of pottery look best with a natural clay appearance, but generally you will prefer to glaze your wares. Glaze provides a sealed surface that is non-porous and in which the clay is dressed over with a bonded film of glass-like material which is easy to clean, smooth to the touch and

3 Brush the slaked glaze through a fine sieve to achieve a completely homogenous fluid.

4 Test the consistency of the glaze by briefly dipping a bisque fired tile into the slip.

5 Attach a fired test sample to glaze bucket. Make a note of details and code base of test.

decorative.

Glaze itself may be thought of as a precise mixture of chemicals that, under a controlled application of heat to a given level, form a predetermined type of glass.

It is normally applied to the bisque fired pot as a suspension of the chemical particles in water (called a glaze slip). The ware is sufficiently porous to absorb the water out of this mixture, leaving a deposit of chemicals on the pot's surface.

The first task is to buy or prepare the basic glaze mixture, considering certain factors.

The maturation temperature

This must be comfortably within the capability of the kiln to be used to fire it. It must also relate to the clay used to form the pot. Earthenware clay pots must be glazed with an earthenware glaze. Pots made with a stoneware clay body will normally be glazed with a stoneware glaze, but the lower temperature earthenware glazes may be used.

Glazes with differing characteristics may be used on a single pot providing that they all have the same maturation temperature.

Surface

The two most common glaze surfaces are glossy and matt, although there is a range of possibilities between these two extremes. There are also special surfaces suitable for larger pieces and sculpture.

Transparency

Glazes are normally either transparent or opaque. Transparent glazes are used with decorative effects such as mishima (page 46) and slip painting (page 42), which need to be allowed to show through the glaze. Opaque glazes normally mask the clay surface of the pot completely.

Some glazes, such as those using borax as a flux, for example, tend to produce a semi-opaque effect.

Colour

Most glaze bases are, by themselves, colourless or whitish. Any glaze may be coloured by combining appropriate amounts of metallic oxide in the glaze composition. These oxides should be weighed out as a percentage of the total of all the solid glaze components and thoroughly dispersed amongst them before water is added (see page 37).

If you decide to buy a ready prepared glaze you will have little to do other than mix it with water, although you will probably find it advantageous to pass it dry through a sieve first to break down any lumps it may contain.

Alternatively you may decide to compound your own glaze from a recipe. If such should be your intention a brief word of advice here may save you disappointment later.

Glazes are highly variable things. Some components are of uniform chemical composition despite their source; others, particularly naturally occurring components, may differ quite considerably from deposit to deposit. The authors of books you consult probably used their local materials as far as possible and a glaze that worked perfectly for them may require some modification. Some materials may be unobtainable and substititions will have to be made. Unless you have access to experienced advice, therefore, avoid recipes from books which are imprecise as to details of materials required and recommend foreign products that are difficult to obtain.

Having selected an appropriate glaze base and gathered together the component materials, decide how much glaze you want to make. 1,000 g (20 lb) is sufficient for a modest batch of wares. Calculate how much of each material you will need and check your mathematics before you start.

Weigh out a precise amount of each chemical, using an accurate beam scale or balance. If any chemical appears to be even marginally lumpy pass it through a sieve and take your required amount from the sieved material.

6   To glaze small pots, fill with prepared glaze poured from a jug and empty immediately.

7   Grasp the pot by its foot and push down into glaze so that the exterior is coated. Let surplus drip.

8 Decoratively shaped areas of glaze can be achieved on exteriors with angled dippings.

9 Interiors or larger pots can be glazed by swilling with a modest amount of glaze.

10 Use a funnel to intoruce glaze into the interiors of narrow-necked bottles.

11 Wax resist can be applied beneath glaze or between two applications of glaze for decorative effects.

12 The exteriors of pots may be glazed by rotating them in the path of a glaze flow.

13 Pots that cannot be hand held are normally supported on two sticks and glazed by pouring.

Metallic oxides used for colouring are added to the total batch mass of glaze chemicals. If a glaze requires 10 g ($\frac{1}{3}$ oz) oxide as a colourant for a 1,000 g (20 lb) bath of glaze the composition will be 1,000 g (20 lb) base plus 10 g ($\frac{1}{3}$ oz) oxide. You may well need to use a separate balance suited to weighing very small amounts in order to weigh out the colourants accurately

A thorough and even dispersal of all the materials is essential. Do as much as you can to achieve this condition before slaking the glaze with water.

If no mechanical dry mixing equipment is available pass the combined materials three times through a sieve with a hand mixing between each sieving. If the glaze contains any form of raw lead or other toxic material mix by shaking the chemicals together in a closed container.

To start with you will need about 685 ml ($1\frac{1}{4}$ pints) water for each 810 g (1 lb $12\frac{1}{2}$ oz) dry glaze. Place the water in a plastic bucket and sprinkle the dry mixed glaze on its surface. Mix thoroughly until a thin, creamy solution is obtained. Test the mixture on a scrap of fired bisque ware similar to that to be glazed until a brief dipping gives a film about the thickness of thick drawing paper. Mix in additional small amounts of water until this constency is achieved.

It is best to allow the glaze to stand a few hours before use. Mix by hand and brush the glaze through a sieve immediately prior to use.

Scrape down any dry glaze which adheres to the interior surface of the bucket after use into the fluid slip and cover with a lid for storage.

Glaze application

Glaze can be applied to bisque wares by any of a number of techniques. The pot may be covered by a single glaze or additional applications of the same or other glazes may be made onto this initial film for thicker or decorative effects.

Mix the glaze carefully and thoroughly by hand and brush it through a fine sieve. Test the consistency on a scrap of bisque fired ware prior to use; blend in a little additional water if the slip is too thick.

Wash your hands before you handle the wares to make certain that you do not get grease and dirt onto the surface of the pottery.

The standard technique for glazing small pots can be seen in the illustration. First glaze the interior of the pot by filling it with glaze poured from a jug. Empty the glaze back into the glaze bucket immediately. A film of glaze will be left adhering to the inner surface of the pots which will dry rapidly.

Proceed to glaze the exterior of the piece at once. Grasp the inverted pot by the foot and thrust it down into the glaze so that the slip

A fluid glaze is used here over more stable ones to achieve an active and varied effect.

rises up the sides of the form as far as is necessary. Withdraw the pot from the glaze at once and hold it an angle above the glaze bucket (see **7**) while it drains and dries. The final drip of glaze, which tends to hang from the lip, can be drained off by touching it against the wall of the bucket.

The technique of applying glaze with a brush is little used, except to glaze small areas or apply decorative motifs. Should you attempt to glaze large areas in this manner use a large brush well loaded with glaze and apply it with confident, generous strokes.

A large calligraphy brush can be used to overlay brushwork or splashed glaze onto the overall glaze as soon as it has stiffened.

Dramatic effects can occasionally be achieved with just a single momentous splash of glaze on an otherwise unglazed form.

An alternative method of glazing the exterior of forms that can be hand held is to pour glaze over its surface from a jug. This is a good method of glazing shallow dishes, but it can also be used for bowl and cylinder forms. Use a twisting motion of the wrist to turn the pot into the path of the flowing glaze. This method is particularly satisfactory when you wish the appearance of the glaze application itself to have an intrinsically decorative and organic quality.

Pots which are unusually absorbent are difficult to glaze, since the body dries out the glaze and prevents its flow. Bodies that contain considerable amounts of grog or sand or are highly absorbent should, therefore, be slaked by brief immersion in clean water prior to glazing. Proceed to glaze as soon as the surface is dry.

Forms which are large can have their interiors glazed by pouring in a comparatively small amount of glaze and rotating the piece so that the moving glaze eventually coats all parts of the inner surface.

The exterior of large, heavy or difficult to hold forms is most easily glazed if the pot is stood on wooden slats above a bowl to catch surplus glaze. Stand the bowl on a banding wheel and turn slowly to feed the surface of the pot into the path of the glaze flow.

When glazing narrow-necked forms, such as bottles, use a funnel to direct the glaze into the interior. This prevents an excessive build-up of glaze in the neck areas as well as simplifying the filling of the form.

Wax resist may be applied onto the glaze film as soon as it has dried and the pot re-glazed with a glaze of contrasting colour to produce a two-colour effect.

GLOST FIRING

You will need:
Equipment listed on page 49

In most cases the temperature achieved during a glaze firing will be considerably higher than that of the earlier bisque firing.

Brush out or vacuum the kiln, taking particular care to remove all fragments of clay from elements and element housings.

Select the appropriate kiln shelves for the proposed temperature. Check that they are sound and unwarped.

Repair the film of bat wash on shelves, if necessary; clean off sides and brush down reverse of each shelf.

Check that you have enough sound refractory shelf props of suitable dimension.

Set the floor shelves in place on low refractory props (see page 50).

Preparing the pots
The pots to be fired may now be prepared. Although they may be covered with a wide variety of glazes, they must all have a common temperature. Thus, glaze firings (or 'glost' firings, as they are usually known) are normally referred to as being, for example, 'a cone four firing', which means that all the wares in the kiln have glazes which mature at the kiln condition indicated by the bending of cone four.

Pots for firing should have been allowed to stand between the application of glaze and packing into the kiln so that the water absorbed from the glaze has had a chance to evaporate. However, all pots will contain some moisture.

Clean off any glaze from the foot-ring of the pot which would come into contact with the kiln shelf. If this were not done its melting to a glass during firing and its subsequent cooling would bond the pot solidly to the shelf or, indeed, anything else it touches. Also, since the glaze is fluid at its maturation temperature, it tends to run slightly down the walls of the pot; consequently, it is advisable to clean the glaze from about 2.5 mm (1/10 in.) of the wall above the actual foot.

Pots that have a flat base and no distinct foot as such should have the whole base cleaned of glaze.

Use a moist sponge to clean the glaze from the foot of the pot.

The basic rules to remember in packing glazed wares into an electric kiln prior to firing are:

1 Pots must not touch one another, although the gaps between them need to be only very small.
2 Geometric and flat-sided forms, such as slab ports, should be fired near the centre of the kiln to prevent them warping or splitting.
3 There must be a gap between the pots and kiln elements and between pots, kiln walls and thermocouple.
4 All shelves must be supported upon refractory props located vertically above those below.
5 Kiln shelves must not touch the electric elements, or directly face an element if an alternative position is possible.
6 The density of the kiln pack should be kept as even as possible.
7 Do not handle the pots unnecessarily.

Sort the pots to be fired into

groups depending upon their height. Alternate the size of the gaps between the shelves to help equalize the density. Choose an appropriate number of refractory props to go with each group. The props should be about 6-12 mm ($\frac{1}{4}$-$\frac{1}{2}$ in.) taller than the height of the highest pot in the group.

Start packing the empty kiln from the back. Place the rear refractory prop(s) in place first, then set any geometric slab pots to be included in this first layer of the pack in place along the centre of the shelf equidistant from the elements. Fill in the remainder of the space, working forwards from the back of the chamber, with whichever pots can be most economically used. Set the front refractory props in position before filling in the space around them.

Lift the next shelf into the kiln and lower it down onto the props, making certain that in so doing you have not tilted one of them out of its vertical position. Check that none of the pots is touching the underside of the shelf. A stepped relationship between the back and front stacks of shelves in deep or large kilns helps to facilitate heat penetration.

Any pots which have glaze close to the base or which have on them a glaze which tends to be more than usually fluid should be raised off the kiln shelf on special kiln furniture (**4**, page 50).

The plaque of pyrometric cones must be placed within the kiln at a point where the whole plaque may be observed through the kiln's peephole. (In large kilns use a plaque of cones opposite each peephole.) Do not set the cones so that they will come into contact with pots as they bend.

Fill the whole kiln and finally re-check that you can see the cones when the kiln door is closed.

14 Before taking glazed wares to the kiln, check that bases are free of glaze. Wipe off with moist sponge.

15 Set individual pots on refractory props for the glaze firing if the glazes have a tendency to run.

16 Set glazed pots so that they do not touch one another or sides of kiln. Avoid wastage of space.

Firing cycle
Lock the kiln door shut and remove bungs from the peepholes in the door. (Some kilns have additional bungs at the top and/or back and these may also be removed.) Raise the kiln temperature very slowly to 100°C (212°F) and allow the kiln to stand at this temperature for about an hour to drive out atmospheric and absorbed moisture. Temperature may now be raised by as much as 100°C (212°F) in each hour for regular pottery – slower firing is desirable for thick wares or sculptural pieces.

Replace all kiln bungs when 200°C (392°F) has been passed.

Cut back the rate of temperature rise when the kiln is approaching the maturation temperature of the glaze and, in large kilns, adjust the energy regulator controls as necessary to achieve an equalization of temperature throughout the kiln.

During the last few degrees of temperature the rate of increase should be as slow as can be managed. Maintain the maturation temperature for about one hour. This period of soak allows all gases to escape from the glaze and all the resulting blemishes to run smooth.

When the period of soak is completed power may be disconnected and the kiln should be allowed to cool in its completely sealed state. The process of cooling must not be hurried if dunting of the wares is to be avoided. Do not, in any event, attempt to break the seal on the kiln till 200°C (392°F) has been reached and then only open the door about 25 mm (1 in.) at first.

The vast majority of your wares should have fired perfectly, but do not be discouraged by a few faults – it is quite normal.

The Sawdust Kiln

1 Lay out the foundation course. This may consist of 8 or 12 bricks depending on capacity required.

2 Build to full height. Allow slightly larger gaps between bricks in foundation and upper courses.

3 Pour in sawdust base and load pots in layers with bed of sawdust between each layer.

You will need:
7-12 courses of 12 common
 building bricks
Sawdust
Fuel-soaked sacking

The sawdust kiln is one of the simplest and least expensive methods of firing pottery. It produces marvellously rich and varied colour effects and the materials for its use are easily available. Its construction and firing method are so basic that the kiln is well within the capabilities of anyone.

Sawdust kilns are constructed from common building bricks and may be located in any open outdoor space. One of the advantages of sawdust kilns is that very little heat is transmitted to the exterior of the kiln, which means that they can be built and used safely in schools. Sawdust kilns do, in fact, bring pottery and a firing method within the capability of any school, even the most elementary, and any house with a garden.

The average sawdust kiln is constructed from about 90 common building bricks. These are assembled in a loose construction – no mortar, fire cement or any other kind of seal being used between the bricks.

Build the kiln on a piece of flat ground. Lay out the base layer of bricks on the ground, as shown, with the bricks placed on their sides and having their frogs facing inwards. Each wall of an average sized kiln is three and a half bricks in length, giving a total of 12 bricks for each course. Allow a gap of about 6 mm ($\frac{1}{4}$ in.) between each brick unless you are siting the kiln in an extremely sheltered location, when you may find this gap has to be increased somewhat.

The kiln may be between seven and 12 courses of bricks in height, depending upon the number of pots to be fired. Leave 25 mm (1 in.) gaps between the bricks on the top layer.

Fill the bottom 20 cm (8 in.) of the kiln with sawdust, which may be obtained cheaply by the sack from any woodyard. (One large sack of sawdust is usually sufficient for a firing.) Place the first layer of pots, which must be thoroughly dry, mouth upwards, directly upon this mound. Leave at least 50 mm (2 in.) between each pot and the walls of the kiln.

4 Light kiln from the top with fuel-soaked sacking. Get sawdust burning briskly before covering.

5 After firing is completed you will find the fired pots in the ash at the base of the kiln.

This first layer of pots should consist of the largest and heaviest to be fired. All pots included in the firing should be filled with sawdust except for bottles or forms with narrow necks.

Cover the first layer of pots with 5 cm (2 in.) sawdust and add the second layer of wares. Continue in this manner until the topmost tier, consisting of the lightest pots, has been packed. Twelve to 20 pots constitute an average packing. Cover the top layer of pots with 30 cm (12 in.) sawdust. There should be two or more courses of brick above the top surface of the sawdust.

The kiln is lit from the top, using a reasonably large piece of old sacking soaked in paraffin or waste sump oil. Lay the soaked sacking on top of the sawdust and cover most of it with a thin layer, 6-12 mm ($\frac{1}{4}$-$\frac{1}{2}$ in.), of sawdust. Leave the corners of the sacking uncovered and ignite them to start the kiln. As the sawdust on top of the sacking catches fire sprinkle some some additional fuel on top of it until a good intensity of heat is produced across the whole surface.

The kiln may now be covered over with a metal lid, as shown, or with a paving slab or kiln shelf, and in most instances requires no further attention until firing is complete.

The kiln tends to emit some flame between the top layers of bricks for about half an hour, after which smoke is emitted. The amount of smoke released decreases significantly after the first hour. If flames continue after the stated time it is probably due to wind activity and gaps between alternate bricks in the wall facing the wind should be plugged with a mixture of clay and sand or grog.

The sawdust smoulders downwards through the kiln, firing the pots as it comes to them. You can easily tell how far down the kiln firing has progressed by testing the exterior wall with your hands.

The kiln may take anything between 12 and 36 hours to fire, depending upon the type of sawdust and the atmospheric conditions. A pile of wares will then be found deposited in the bottom of the kiln. These normally feature the varied and attractive effects of contact with direct fire.

For use in schools it is recommended that a second wall with larger – 50 mm (2 in.) – gaps between the bricks be constructed around the whole kiln at a distance of 150 mm (6 in.) from it and that the slab type of cover be used instead of the metal lid, which does become rather hot.

You may increase the temperature achieved within the sawdust kiln somewhat by burning a brisk wood fire between the kiln and this outer wall. Start the fire after the kiln has been lit an hour, burn for an hour and repeat at two-hourly intervals.

Wares to be fired in sawdust kilns should be of an open textured type of clay containing reasonable amounts (20% or more) of grog and/or sand. Although less open wares can be fired in sawdust kilns they are more frequently subject to damage.

Unusually tall wares do not fire well in sawdust kilns and should in any case be packed horizontally.

Enamels and Beads

1 Use a palette knife to mix enamel and fat oil to a creamy consistency on a glass slab.

2 Grind the mixture into a smooth paste by a rotary action with a glass mortar.

3 Bisque fire pots with lids in place and bowls prone to distortion on their lips.

You will need:
Enamels in powder form
Palette knife
Oil
Glass slab
Mortar
White spirit
Clay
Knife
Straw
Emery paper
Slips
Nichrome wire
Glazes

Most pots are considered complete after glazing, but you can still apply further decoration in the form of on-glaze enamels. Ceramic enamel is simply a very low temperature glaze which is painted onto the existing fired glaze surface. Once the enamel has dried the pot has to be given a further firing, which both fuses the enamel to a glass and also bonds it to the underlying glazed surface.

Although enamels can, in theory, be applied to most glazed wares, the base glaze must not be re-melted when firing on the enamels. Enamel decoration is more normally applied onto stoneware and porcelain than onto earthenware, but the process is perfectly applicable to this latter case provided that the subsequent firing is carefully controlled.

Enamel decoration is at its most effective when applied on a plain and featureless base glaze, usually a plain opaque white.

Enamels are usually designed to fuse at 730-800°C (1346-1472°F). They may be coloured with stains or oxides, exactly as glazes are. The most sophisticated enamelled wares are given several firings but it is unlikely that you will want to undertake more than one enamel firing.

4 Form blanks individually or cut lengths from an extruded coil. Push a straw through centre of each.

5 Refine the shape of the beads with tools or on a piece of abrasive paper.

6 Colour areas of the surface with slips of underglaze colours. Bisque fire when dry.

7 A simple, slab-built firing frame for beads. Thread them on heat-resistant nichrome wire.

On-glaze enamels (sometimes also called china paints) can be bought prepared and ready for use from most ceramics suppliers. A very wide range of stable, strong colours are available.

Enamels are economical and you need buy only very small amounts. They are compounded into a fluid material by adding either a liquid medium (sold with the enamels) or a glaze gum solution. Mix powder and medium together to get a paint-like consistency. Many potters like to use a glass muller and slab for this mixing process and, indeed, the grinding together of the two materials does seem to improve the workability of the mixture. It should be neither so glutinous that it cannot be applied smoothly nor so fluid that it runs down the form.

Apply the enamel directly with a brush or draw outlines of motifs with a volatile crayon and fill in with enamel. The crayon will burn away during firing.

Fire to the temperature recommended by the manufacturer. Fire the kiln with door peepholes and vents open up to 500°C (932°F). The temperature rise should be very slow up to this point, as the gum has to be burned out of the enamel. Too rapid a rise in temperature will cause the enamel film to peel.

If possible, soak the kiln at the maturation tempetrature of the enamel for about twenty minutes before cooling very slowly.

Making the beads

Extremely attractive ceramic beads are easy to make. They are best made with white clay and coloured with oxides, stains and glazes.

Take a well kneaded clay body which contains up to 20% fine grog and roll into thin, even coils; cut with a sharp knife.

Push a piece of dry grass through the centre of each bead and allow to dry. Once dry, remove the grass and refine the shape of the bead with glasspaper or fine files.

Slip decoration may be applied at this stage. Make the slip up to a thin consistency and apply several coats with a brush.

Beads are most easily bisque fired together inside any convenient pot.

Since beads cannot be effectively glaze fired by normal placement in the kiln a special firing frame needs to be constructed, as illustrated. Make the frame by the slab building method from well grogged clay and bisque fire it.

Paint the beads with stains, oxides and glaze in whatever patterns and colours are required. Make certain that the penetrations through the centres of the beads are free of glaze.

Thread the beads onto lengths of nichrome wire and attach to the firing frame, as shown. Make certain that the beads do not touch one another.

The frame may now be loaded in the conventional manner into an appropriate glaze firing.

Storage and Reconstitution of Clay

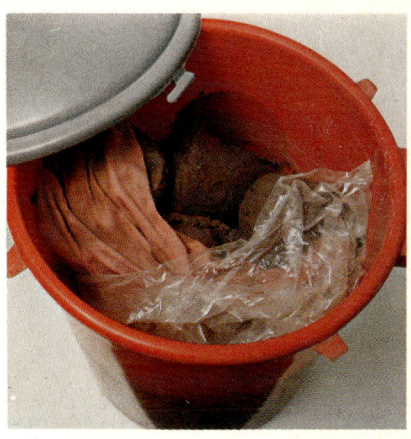

1 Dry, unfired clay may be reconstituted and make workable by simply submerging it in water.

2 When the clay has slaked down, spread it on plaster until stiff enough to knead.

3 Store clay in kneaded masses, wrapped in damp cloth, in a lidded container (plastic is ideal).

You will need:
Buckets of water
Plaster slab or dish mould
Damp cloths
Lidded containers

Any pottery studio has two accumulations of clay other than that for immediate use: a general stock of clay and scrap clay. Your general stock needs to be stored carefully, while the second needs to be recycled.

New clay is normally supplied in sealed plastic bags and will remain in good working condition. The clay you are going to use, together with similar recycled clay, can be stored in bins of a good size with close-fitting lids.

Cut the clay into fairly large lumps and give it a preliminary kneading. Cover all the clay in the bin with a wet cloth and a piece of plastic sheeting before closing the bin. Keep separate bins for each sort of plastic clay you buy and store grogged clay separately.

Scrap clay is normally fairly plastic, leather-hard or dry. Sprinkle plastic clay with a little water and return it to the stock.

Submerge dry scrap clay in a bin of water, cover and allow to stand till it has slaked down to the constituency of soft mud. Spread this onto a large slab of plaster or put into large plaster dish moulds. Turn the clay after a few hours. Knead back into working condition the following day.

Alternatively, pound dry clay into small fragments and put them into a plastic container. Sprinkle with water, cover with damp sacking and seal the container. Turn the clay next day and sprinkle on more water. Repeat until the clay has reabsorbed sufficient water.

Leather-hard clay is best reconstituted by drying it out first.

List of suppliers

Great Britain

British Ceramic Service Co. Ltd
Bricesco House
1 Park Avenue
Wolstanton
Staffs

Ferro (GB) Ltd
Wombourne
Wolverhampton

Fulham Pottery
210 Kings Road
London SW6

Pike Brothers
Wareham
Dorset

W. Podmore & Sons Ltd
Caledonia Mills
Shelton
Stoke-on-Trent
Staffs

Potclays Ltd
Wharf House
Copeland Street
Hanley
Stoke-on-Trent
Staffs

USA

Alaska Mud Puddle
9034 Hartzell Road
Anchorage
Alaska 99502

American Art Clay Co.
4717 W. 16 Street
Indianapolis
Indiana 46222

Capital Ceramics
2174 S. Main Street
Salt Lake City
Utah 84115

Cedar Heights Clay Co.
Oak Hill
Ohio 45656

Ceramic Colour & Chemical
Manufacturing Co.
Box 297
New Brighton
Pennsylvania 15066

Ceramics-Hawaii Ltd
629 Cooke Street
Honolulu
Hawaii 96813

Dec Ceramics
2401 East 40th Ave
Denver
Colorado 80205

Ferro Corporation
4150 East 56th Street
Cleveland
Ohio 44105

General Refractories Co.
7640 West Chicago Ave
Detroit
Michigan 48204

Hammell & Gillespie Inc.
255 Broadway
New York
N.Y. 10007

O. Hommel Co.
Hope Street
Carnegie
Pennsylvania 15106

Pemco Corporation
5601 Easten Ave
Baltimore
Maryland 21202

Standard Ceramic Supply Co.
Box 4435
Pittsburgh
Pennsylvania 15205

Terra Ceramics
3035 Koapako Street
Honolulu
Hawaii 96819

Van Howe Ceramic Supply Co.
4216 Edith N.E.
Albuquerque
New Mexico 87107

Western Ceramics Supply Co.
1601 Howard Street
San Francisco
California 94103

Some further reading

Ceramics – a potter's handbook
G.C. Nelson, Holt, Reinhard &
Winston, New York, 1964

Clay and Glazes for the Potter
Daniel Rhodes, Chilton,
Philadelphia, 1957; Pitman, London, 1958

An Illustrated Dictionary of Practical Pottery R. Fournier, Van
Nostrand Reinhold, New York
and London, 1974

A Manual of Pottery and Ceramics
David Hamilton, Thames & Hudson, London, 1974; Van Nostrand
Reinhold, New York

Pottery Making – a complete guide
John Dickerson, Nelson, London,
1974; Viking, New York

Technique of Pottery D.M.
Billington, Batsford, London,
1962; Hearthside, New York

Acknowledgement

Pyrometer, thermocouple and kiln
supplied by courtesy of Fulham
Pottery, London (Page 49 and 51).

738.1 P85   93133

POTTERY STEP-BY-STEP

College Misericordia Library
Dallas, Pennsylvania 18612